NEEDLE FELTING

THROUGH *the* SEASONS

NEEDLE FELTING
THROUGH *the* SEASONS

12 Beginner Projects for the Home

ELIZABETH WHITTON

SCHIFFER CRAFT
4880 Lower Valley Road • Atglen, PA 19310

For my family: Joshua, Grace, and Rue, and my parents, George and Nancy. Without you I wouldn't be a needle felting artist, business owner, or author. Thank you for always supporting me.

Special thanks to Amy Kimball, who took every one of the beautiful photos in this book and also let me include images of her farm and sheep.

Other Schiffer Craft Books on Related Subjects:

Jaana Mattson's Landscapes in Wool: The Art of Needle Felting, Jaana Mattson, ISBN 978-0-7643-6126-5

Felting, Elvira López Del Prado Rivas, ISBN 978-0-7643-4531-9

Library of Congress Control Number: 2026932939

Designed by Michael Douglas
Front cover design by Lindsay Hess
Photography by Amy Kimball
Edited by Kaylee Schofield
Type set in Adriane Text and Muli

ISBN: 978-0-7643-7244-5
ePub: 978-1-5073-0762-5
Printed in China
10 9 8 7 6 5 4 3 2 1

MIX
Paper | Supporting responsible forestry
FSC www.fsc.org FSC® C167893

Published by Schiffer Craft
An imprint of Schiffer Publishing, Ltd.
4880 Lower Valley Road
Atglen, PA 19310
Phone: (610) 593-1777; Fax: (610) 593-2002
Email: Info@schifferbooks.com
Web: www.schifferbooks.com

For our complete selection of fine books on this and related subjects, please visit our website at www.schifferbooks.com. You may also write for a free catalog.

Schiffer Publishing's titles are available at special discounts for bulk purchases for sales promotions or premiums. Special editions, including personalized covers, corporate imprints, and excerpts, can be created in large quantities for special needs. For more information, contact the publisher.

We are always looking for people to write books on new and related subjects. If you have an idea for a book, please contact us at proposals@schifferbooks.com.

Contents

Felted Sky
www.feltedsky.com

What Is Needle Felting?

Needle felting is the art of poking fluffy sheep's wool with a special type of barbed needle. Wool fibers contain microscopic scales, and the repetitive stabbing motion of the needle causes these to tangle and lock together. As you poke and jab, the wool becomes firmer and can be sculpted into nearly any shape. Projects with multiple pieces are joined using only the wool and needle. No sewing or glue is required! It's a bit like magic that way.

In flat projects, dyed wool is stabbed into a backing, and you can create pictures that have layers of texture and color. This has come to be known as "painting with wool." If you're putting wool on a printed pattern or drawing, I like to call that "coloring with wool," because it is a little like paint-by-number, filling in coloring books, or working with embroidery and cross-stitch patterns.

Hybrid needle felting projects combine both 2-D and 3-D techniques together in the same piece, with interesting and appealing results. Needle felting can also be incorporated into mixed-media artwork. It can be used in the same finished pieces with wet felting, embroidery, punch needle, weaving, and more! There are so many creative ways to use it.

Needle felting is a fairly simple and accessible technique to learn (just stabbing!). It also tends to be a very calming and stress-relieving art form. The tactile nature of the wool, the beautiful colors, and the repetitive motion can make it almost meditative. While there are very detailed and advanced projects that can take a lot of time to create, many small beginner projects can be finished in a few hours.

My focus in my needle felting business, and now, in this book, has been to design beautiful projects that aren't too time-consuming and can fit into a busy lifestyle. I like to make things that have a place and a purpose and can be displayed in the home, either on the walls and furniture or as holiday decorations. Modern life is busy and stressful for most of us, but I find that it helps me slow down and find more gratitude and ease if I take time for crafting and make the changing of the seasons a little bit special.

I hope you come to love needle felting as much as I do, and that the projects in this book bring you joy and excitement about what you can create with your own two hands, some wool, and a needle.

Happy felting!

3-D SCULPTURES

Making little sculptures used to be the most popular type of needle felting. There are many crafters and artists who have focused on making animals, which can be either amazingly realistic or cute and stylized. Seasonal decorations such as eggs, pumpkins, and ornaments are also very prevalent in the world of needle felting. But you can turn wool into whatever you can dream up, in whatever style best suits you! Needle felting is being used now in stop-motion animation and in huge modern sculptures that are displayed in galleries and public places. My own 3-D work has focused on flowers, plants, and, of course, holiday decorations.

2-D PICTURES

Flat needle felting has come a long way in the past decade and is quickly catching up with sculpting in popularity. Some notable artists have pushed the limits and taken the craft into the realm of fine art. Lifelike pet portraits have become especially well loved. Needle felting can also be used on functional objects such as pillows, bags, felted slippers, and even clothing. With the current widespread interest in visible mending, needle-felted designs can play a part in filling in holes and covering stains. As with sculpture, needle-felted pictures can be made in any style and size. My own 2-D work, like my sculpting, is full of landscapes, plants, and flowers but also includes the occasional decorative pillow.

▲ While more time-consuming, sometimes it's fun to go big! This 24" x 36" landscape hangs in my living room.

▲ This is my most popular landscape kit, inspired by rolling hills and fertile fields. It seems only fitting to create sheep out of wool fibers!

▲ I like working from photos of stunning places and figuring out how to simplify them into teachable steps while retaining their beauty.

▲ Layers are the key to my landscapes. This one starts with background colors of sky, water, and sand. Then you add clouds, land, trees, etc.

▲ This picture was imagined. I combined mountains, rock formations, and cacti from different places to make a coherent scene.

HYBRID PIECES

This is an up-and-coming approach to needle felting that combines 2-D and 3-D elements in the same piece. I find the possibilities very exciting. Here are two of my hybrid works.

NEEDLE FELTING IN MIXED MEDIA

Combining needle felting with other fiber arts offers so many interesting possibilities. You can add needle-felted elements—either flat or sculptural—to woven wall hangings. You can add stitching or beads (or both) on top of needle-felted pictures or sculptures. Here are two examples.

Cherry wood box courtesy of www.camdenrose.com

THE Basics

Most of us grew up knowing a little bit about the more common fiber arts such as knitting, crochet, or cross-stitch because we saw people around us doing those things. When I am out in the world and asked what I do for a living, I still come across many people who have never heard of needle felting and don't have any direct experience of it. Because of that, it can feel somewhat daunting when you're just getting started. In this section, I give a basic overview of what you'll need to know to be successful in your needle felting journey.

Supplies and Terminology

Needle felting has its own jargon, especially when it comes to describing different types of wool and felting needles. It can be overwhelming at first to navigate the world of felting supplies. If you're new to the craft and don't have a local teacher or shop to answer your questions, the following pages should help you to determine what supplies you'll need and how to search for them, especially if you are shopping online. You could also start with a kit, which will have everything in it that you'll need to make a specific project. In fact, kits are the cornerstone of my business because they make it easy for anyone to jump right in and get felting.

WOOL

Wool is a very important part of needle felting. There are many different types of wool, so it can be hard to know what to purchase when you're just getting started. The right kind of wool can make needle felting easier and a finished piece more beautiful. The wrong kind of wool can make the process more challenging and the finished piece less appealing. I always recommend sheep's wool for needle felting, even though most animal fibers will "felt" to some degree.

Sheep's wool is classified on the basis of the length of the hair fibers themselves (called staple length), the diameter of the individual fibers (called micron count), and the crimp of the fiber (the amount of waviness in it). In general, I prefer to work with wool that has a "short" staple length (2–4 inches) and a micron count in the "medium" range (22–27 microns). It usually works better if it has some crimp to it. While those characteristics are ideal, wool that falls outside these ranges can also work. Trial and error is your best bet when trying out different types of wool.

Wool is usually sold by weight. You will be purchasing wool in ounces in the US and grams in other parts of the world. Purchasing wool from small businesses that specialize in needle felting or fiber arts will usually make felting easier from the get-go. I also love to encourage people to go to fiber festivals, where you can purchase wool directly from small farms. These annual events are scattered all over the United States and are well worth visiting. You can also check for needle felting wool and supplies at your local yarn shop.

3
2
5
1
4
3

TERMINOLOGY

1. **Batting** is a rectangular sheet of fiber that is made on a carding machine. It is the preparation of wool that I reach for the most. You can easily cover large areas with a uniform amount of wool, but you can also pull off small bits from an end. You can easily tear it into different sizes and shapes on the basis of what you want to make.

2. **Roving** is a general term for a long, continuous rope of wool fiber. It can also be called "top" or "sliver," depending on its preparation. It can also be used to cover an area with color, but you will generally need to overlap more pieces of it than when using batting. It lends itself to making thin lines, landscape elements such as tree trunks or grasses, and realistic hair and fur.

3. **Core wool** refers to any wool that you use on the inside of a sculpture. It can be prepared as roving or batting. It is usually undyed and less expensive than what you use for your "top coat" of dyed wool that will show on the outside of the finished piece. I prefer batting for most projects, but roving can work better for wrapping wire.

4. **Wool locks** are the curly hair of longwool sheep breeds. They often have great luster and can vary a lot in length and tightness of the curls. These can be incorporated into needle-felted artwork and are sometimes used for foliage or for realistic-looking hair on figures and animals.

5. **Wool nepps** are tiny bits of wool that are a byproduct of wool carding. They can be incorporated into needle-felted work when you need a lot of little dots or to give extra texture.

STORAGE

I recommend thinking about how you want to store your wool. In some places and in some houses, there may be insects (such as wool moths) that lay eggs in animal fibers. When the larvae hatch, they eat through the fiber. This is why our mothers and grandmothers carefully stored their furs and wool sweaters in cedar chests and closets to deter those little pests. I have rarely had to deal with moths, but the occasional infestation has taught me to be careful. Minimally processed and undyed small-farm wool may pose the most risk because it has not gone through the high temperatures of the dying process. If you do ever see evidence of moths or their larvae in your wool, it is usually best to discard it and start again fresh. If you want to try to salvage the wool, putting it in the freezer for a few days should kill any eggs or larvae.

To head off this problem, I recommend storing your wool in closed plastic bags, at the very least. Various plastic bins and plastic craft organizers with lids can also work well. Glass jars are another very good-looking solution. If you are confident that moths are not an issue in your house or with the wool you are using, a hanging shoe organizer can be a fun and inexpensive way to organize your wool.

Be warned that pets such as cats and dogs usually also love wool. If they have access to it and are not trained to leave it alone, they may try to steal it and play with it, leaving it in a big, slobbery, unusable mess. One of our puppies loved to steal balls of wool from a room she wasn't supposed to be in when she thought we weren't paying attention! This is another good reason to store your wool away in closed containers.

Our wool thief!

NEEDLES

Felting needles are made for industry and intended to be used in large machines, moving only straight up and down, to manufacture all kinds of nonwoven fabrics and materials. It has been only in the past few decades that needle felting has gained popularity as an art form. This is why felting needles bend and break easily—because they are not designed for this purpose or to withstand sideways pressure. It is always a good idea to keep some extra needles on hand in case you need to replace one (or a few!) in the middle of a project. This is just a part of needle felting. As you practice more and hone your felting skills, you will learn to break fewer needles.

Like other needles, felting needles are numbered based on their size (also called gauge). The needles used for needle felting range from 32 at the largest to 42 at the smallest. The needles themselves look the same and are usually 3 inches long. It is only the "working part" of the needle, near the tip, that varies in thickness. There are also different types of needles, with names based on the shape of the working part of the needle. The types are triangle, twisted (also called spiral), star, and reverse. The working part of the needle contains "barbs," which are tiny notches that cause the wool fibers to tangle and lock together. The number of barbs on each needle and their placement also vary and will make a difference in how a needle functions.

In general, you use larger needles (denoted by lower numbers) to start shaping sculptures because those needles will felt faster, with more "oomph." Once your shape is established and you want to finish and smooth the surface, you can switch to a finer needle (denoted by higher numbers). Puncture holes always show in a finished piece, but they are much less noticeable when you're using a finer needle. Fine needles are also used for making small parts, but you want to switch to a larger needle for attaching the parts together. For making flat pictures, a medium or "general" gauge of needle (such as a size 38) is usually used.

It can be a little confusing at first to understand the differences in felting needles and what kinds are best suited to the projects you have in mind. While there are around a dozen needles commonly used in needle felting, it is not necessary to try them all unless you want to. The projects in this book are worked with only four needles: a 38 Triangle, 38 Twisted, 38 Star, and 42 Triangle.

HOW TO HOLD A FELTING NEEDLE

Grip the middle of the needle with your thumb and middle finger. Put the top of the needle under your pointer finger or rest your pointer finger on the top of the needle. Having a ring finger on the needle can also be helpful. This grip is usually comfortable and supports the needle in such a way that you'll hopefully break fewer of them.

FINGER GUARDS

These are optional but can be helpful and necessary if you find that you are often poking yourself. Finger guards are long thimbles that are worn on your nondominant hand, usually on your thumb and index finger, but they can be worn on any finger that you tend to poke. There are many options available, from leather to silicone. My favorite type is a fairly thick suede leather. I find these to be protective while allowing a decent range of motion. A strong stab can sometimes still puncture thin leather finger guards. Silicone and rubber are other options. They offer the most protection because they are not easy to puncture but feel bulkier when you're wearing them, allowing a little less range of motion.

4
3
2
1

TOOLS

While needle felting tools are not necessary, and I still do most of my felting holding a single needle in my fingers, there are times when it is nice to use a tool. Tools can be made of plastic, wood, or metal. Keep in mind that needles bend and break in tools just as easily as (if not more often than) when you're felting with a single needle. When you need to replace needles in a tool, most require needles that are unpainted. Painted needles (from color coding) usually don't fit into tools. I prefer to put 38 Star needles in most of my tools, or a fine needle such as a 42 Triangle, if I want to use the tool for surface smoothing. You can experiment with putting different types of needles into your tools.

REASONS TO USE A TOOL

Speed

Because most tools can hold more than one needle—up to eight and beyond—you can felt faster than with a single needle. If you have limited time for crafting, are making anything particularly large, or decide to start selling finished artwork, it can be helpful to felt more quickly. I like to use a tool for shaping large sculptures and for quickly putting on large areas of a single color. I usually switch back to a single needle as soon as I want to work on crisp edges or small details.

Comfort

Tools are available in different shapes and with different grips, and some are made to hold a single needle. If you have arthritis or other health conditions that give you hand pain or fatigue, a tool can be a good solution. Find one that helps your hand and fingers be more comfortable when you're felting.

TYPES OF TOOLS

1. Tools that hold a single needle can make felting more comfortable.

2. Tools that hold a few needles close together are useful for shaping small sculptures and creating "wool paintings."

3. Tools that restrict how far the needles can stab into the piece are usually good for smoothing surfaces, be they flat or 3-D.

4. Tools that hold four to eight needles spaced farther apart are useful for shaping large sculptures or tacking down large areas of color on flat pieces.

Mechanical tools can help you felt even faster! These are either battery-operated or plug in with a cord. I don't personally like the vibration or noise of using a mechanical needle felting tool, but if you want to do a LOT of needle felting and you like machines or have a significant amount of hand fatigue, you might want to try one.

4
5
2
2
3
4
1

WORK SURFACES

Most needle felting projects will be done on a particular type of work surface that we call a "mat." For most projects, the needle needs to be able to poke through the wool and down into the mat. The main exception is if you are working on a sculpture that is big enough that the needle won't poke through it.

There are different types of work surfaces that can be used, on the basis of your personal preferences and what type of felting you want to do. You may want to have different work surfaces for different types of projects. These are the most commonly used mats:

1. **Wet-Felted Wool** This is my favorite work surface because it lasts a long time through many projects and can be used both for sculpting and making flat pictures. I love wool, so why not use it for my work surface too? It does take a little more force to poke into a wool mat than most foam mats. For this reason, you may still want to consider a foam mat as your primary work surface if you have any joint pain or muscle fatigue when you are felting.

2. **Foam** This is my second-favorite work surface. Foam works well and is economical, but it is usually not eco-friendly, and it wears out fairly quickly. For most projects, you can use a foam mat five to ten times per side before it starts breaking down too much and has to be replaced. There are many types of foam, but I prefer a firm foam that is still easy to poke into. The type that I use is high-density open-cell polyurethane foam. It is usually gray or dark charcoal (almost black) in color. White polyethylene foam is another type you may see. Some people also like to felt on foam insulation board. I don't recommend using soft upholstery or mattress-style foam. A firm work surface is better for needle felting.

3. **Commercial Wool Felt** These mats are usually a little thinner and even firmer than wet-felted wool mats. They can be used in the same way, but because they are extra dense, you may want to use a finer needle if you are making 2-D pictures on one, so that it will stab into the felt more easily.

4. **Pillow or Cushion Style** These are commonly made of two layers of burlap fabric and then filled with rice. There are also pillow mats that consist of a felt outer layer filled with wool. This type of mat is usually used for sculpting. Flat pictures are easier to make on the type of foam or wool mats mentioned above.

5. **Bristle Brush** This is another type of work surface for needle felting. Although I don't use them, some people like to make small wool sculptures and shapes on the top of the bristles while the needle goes down into them.

1
2
3
4
5

BACKING FABRICS

While you can try felting onto any fabric, some work better than others for making 2-D pictures. As with most things in needle felting, it is a good practice to experiment and see what you prefer. I work primarily on linen fabric or 100% wool prefelt, but I know other artists who prefer to work exclusively on craft felt.

1. **100% Linen Fabric** This is one of my favorite fabrics to use for felted art. Because linen fabric has a more open weave than woven cotton fabrics, felting needles poke into it fairly easily. Linen fibers are also very strong and can handle lots of poking. A "medium weight" linen in the range of 150–170 gsm (grams per square meter) usually works best. Printed linen fabrics offer intriguing possibilities, but natural or solid colors are more widely used.

2. **Recycled Sweater Felt** This is an eco-friendly and budget-friendly option that can work quite well. If you have old wool sweaters that are past their useful life or you can find 100% wool sweaters at a thrift store, you can run them through the washer and dryer to felt them and then cut them up into pieces to use as backings. If you're not sure whether a sweater will work for this purpose, check the care instructions. If it says "dry clean only" or to wash on delicate and line dry, that usually means it will felt when you wash it. Upcycled sweater felt behaves very similarly to prefelt. It is quite easy to poke into, but it may not hold details as well as linen or craft felt.

3. **Craft Felt** This is another popular option. Craft felt can be made of acrylic, recycled polyester, 100% wool, or wool-and-rayon blends. Felt can take a little more force to poke into than linen fabric or prefelt because it is so dense. However, it is readily available in many colors and it is a good choice for making finely detailed pictures, because it will hold that detail very well. 100% wool felt also looks great if you want to leave your backing showing around a picture.

4. **Prefelt** This material is technically a "preliminary felt," meaning it is in the beginning stages of being turned into felt but it is not all the way there yet. This means it is very easy to poke into with a felting needle, either to manipulate it into different shapes or to add more fibers onto it. If you want to make very detailed wool paintings, you might not want to work on prefelt, because it doesn't hold the wool fibers as tightly as linen or craft felt. Prefelt can be quite thick, such as a ½ inch or more, or very thin. Most prefelt is made from wool fiber, but, like craft felt, it can also be made from other fibers such as recycled plastic, or from blending wool with another type of fiber.

5. **Thick Handmade Felt** This is wet felted from 100% wool and can make a sturdy backing fabric. Being thicker, it probably won't fit into a hoop, but if you're using a different framing or display option, it can be another good choice for a backing material.

3
3
6
5
5
4
4
2
9
2
1
7
8
8

MISCELLANEOUS EXTRAS

1. **Glass Eyes** If you want to create animals or other imaginary creatures with needle felting, you may want to use glass eyes. These usually come on a wire and are available in many different sizes and colors.

2. **Tiny Animal Parts** Some artists create beaks, claws, hooves, and noses out of polymer clay and then add these to their realistic animal sculptures. You may also be able to find ready-made plastic parts such as the noses shown here, along with plastic whiskers. Horsehair can also be purchased as a natural option for making realistic whiskers.

3. **Prefelt or Felt Cutouts** These are usually die-cut on special machines and are fun to decorate. Using a precut shape certainly saves time over cutting them out. While there are many precut felt shapes available on websites such as Etsy, I think that in the future, more thick prefelt shapes will be available as well.

4. **Armatures** When you use wire in needle felting to create a base shape or structure that you wrap wool around, that is called an armature. You could use pipe cleaners, cloth-wrapped wire, or other types of metal wire, from very thin to quite thick. Armatures are often used to make animals with thin, realistic-looking limbs so that they will be able to stand or hold a specific shape. I don't personally use armatures very often, but there are certainly projects where it is necessary.

5. **Wool Blanks** These are shapes premade for needle felting. They are time-savers and can be either needle-felted or wet-felted. Common shapes include eggs and balls. I think that in the future, there will be a larger variety of shapes and sizes available. You usually have to firm and smooth them out a little, but then you can start decorating right away.

6. **Felted Wool Yarn** I use this to make ornament "caps" and pumpkin stems. While I could felt those myself from scratch, it is faster and easier to use this ropelike yarn, which has been wet felted by hand.

7. **Cookie Cutters** An easy way to create flat shapes is by using cookie cutters. Simply fill them with wool and start stabbing! I like to use them for forming petals or leaves. The Citrus Coaster project in this book (page 88) uses a round cookie cutter for its shaping.

8. **Stencils** These can also be useful for needle felting. Stencils made for painting can work, but you may also find them cut out of cardstock or thick felt. The Pine Cone Stocking project in this book (page 136) relies on a stencil to create its design.

9. **Wool Foundations** These are firm shapes made of wool that you felt directly onto, and they become part of the finished piece of art. They are similar to wool mats but a little thinner. They can be handmade (wet felted) or cut from thick, commercially made felt. You can attach sculptural elements to them, or they can become the base for 2-D flat pictures. The Mushrooms and Moss project and Mountain Cabin in this book (pages 98 and 142) both utilize a wool base.

FRAMING AND DISPLAY

There are a few things to consider when you are deciding how to display your needle-felted artwork. I personally like to let the fiber show. I display sculpted pieces out in the open, and flat pictures without any glass on top of them. I know that my artwork may get dusty and the fibers may loosen up and get a little fuzzy, but that's okay with me. If it is a flat piece that is extra important to me, I try to frame it so that I can easily take it out of its frame in a few years and "spruce it up" by dusting it off and poking it more. I like to say, though, that needle-felted art is not like an oil painting. I have some pieces that have been around for 10+ years, and they still look pretty good. They will not last forever, but I will be sure to enjoy them for as long as I can.

OPTIONS FOR 3-D SCULPTURES

If you have pets that might try to steal and destroy your sculptures, or if you create some that you want to take extra-special care of, you may want to display them behind glass. You could either put them into a curio cabinet, into a shadow or display box of some kind, or under a glass cloche. If you decide to leave a sculpture out in the open, just know that you will probably need to brush off the dust and poke it again from time to time.

OPTIONS FOR 2-D PICTURES

One of the easiest and most commonly used ways to frame and display flat pictures is in embroidery hoops. They are economical and widely available. I like to use nice wood hoops when I can, rather than the cheaper versions available at most craft stores. Unlike embroidery or cross-stitch, you need to create flat pieces on a mat and will put them into the hoop only at the end. If you feel that an embroidery hoop isn't quite fancy enough for your art, now there are various types of hoop stands and nice-looking frames that hold embroidery hoops.

Another option is to use a more standard square or rectangular frame. I look for frames that will work with a backer board or already come with one. If the frame came with glass, I take that out, glue my art to the backer board, and put it right into the frame. It is usually easier to find a frame that you like first and make your art to fit into it, rather than to make a piece of artwork and decide after the fact how best to frame it.

One other option is to stretch your work around an artist canvas or simply the stretcher bars that are used for mounting canvases. There are plenty of online tutorials that will show you how to do this. Art that is wrapped around a canvas or stretcher bars can be displayed as is, or you can get a frame for it. Floater frames can look really good—or, if you want to go all out, you could get a custom frame made for your art.

Some people do like to display their flat pictures under glass, either in rectangular frames or shadow boxes. There is nothing wrong with that, and the pieces will certainly be more protected from light, dust, and possible pests. I just personally like to be able to see the texture of a piece without glass in the way.

Frame courtesy of www.modernhoopla.co

COMMON QUESTIONS AND TROUBLESHOOTING

WHAT ARE ALL THE DIFFERENT NEEDLES USED FOR?

32 Triangle: for quick 3-D felting and when you want to make a large or a very firm shape

36 Triangle: for starting a 3-D sculpture, especially ones the size of a fist or larger

38 Triangle: a good "general" needle that can do most everything pretty well

40 Triangle: a general-to-fine needle used most in the finishing stages of sculpting

42 Triangle: for fine detail work, smoothing surfaces, making small parts, and using in tools with closer needle placement

38 Star: my favorite for felting into fabric to make "wool paintings" and for using in tools where needles are spaced farther apart

38 Twisted/Spiral: efficient felting, especially for decorating preformed wool blanks

40 Twisted/Spiral: efficient felting for small parts and surface finishing

Reverse Barb: pulls wool out from previous layers, instead of pushing wool in, for creating realistic whiskers and fur

WHAT DO THE COLORS ON THE NEEDLES MEAN?

Felting needles often come with their ends painted so that you can tell them apart when you have a collection of different ones. Unfortunately, there is not a universal color code, so keep in mind that needles from one seller might be painted different colors than needles from a different seller, even if the sizes and types are the same. It is a good rule of thumb to keep them in their original packaging, so that you know what size and type of needles you have. Needles can vary a lot depending on the manufacturer and placement of the barbs. A 38 Triangle from one seller may felt differently than a 38 Triangle from another. I recommend finding high-quality needles that you like and then continuing to purchase from the same place.

WHY AM I BREAKING SO MANY NEEDLES?

Felting needles can take only a little bit of sideways pressure or torque before they bend and break. Once a needle is bent or broken, it needs to be replaced with a new needle. To break fewer needles, make sure you are poking straight in and straight out. The angle of your stabs can change, but the needle needs to stay straight the whole time. It is when you are trying to drag too much wool into place with the tip of the needle that you get into trouble—or when too much of the needle is embedded in the mat or project when the top of the needle changes directions.

MY NEEDLES ARE RUSTING. WHAT SHOULD I DO?

Felting needles are usually made of high-carbon steel, not stainless steel, so they can eventually develop rust, especially in humid environments. You can wipe rusted needles and continue using them as long as rust isn't rubbing off onto your work. Coating them with a little bit of machine oil can help to prevent rust. As with bent and broken ones, though, you will need to replace rusted needles eventually.

DO FELTING NEEDLES WEAR OUT?

With the amount of time you are needle felting, even if you do a lot of it, felting needles do not generally wear out. In fact, I've never had it happen! You will almost certainly bend or break a needle and have to replace it before it stops working. In industrial applications, where needles might be stabbing a material for many hours a day, day in and day out, wear becomes more of an issue, but it is not an issue with hand felting.

HOW DO I KEEP MY MAT CLEAN?

All mats collect fiber. You can pull off as much as possible in between projects, but eventually there will still be fiber that builds up on the mat. If you are making flat pictures on a backing fabric, the fiber on the mat will not be a problem, because it stays below the fabric. However, having a clean mat is important when you are sculpting. Some people like to divide their mat into sections and felt with certain colors only on certain areas of the mat. For example, one corner of the mat is used for very dark colors. Another part of the mat may be used only for light colors, etc. Another way to get a clean surface is to put down a piece of scrap fabric on the mat and then remove it after you're finished with the project. Some people put down used dryer sheets for this purpose. Scraps of linen fabric, prefelt, or felt also work well.

CAN I FELT WITH OTHER FIBERS?

While sheep's wool works the best for needle felting in my experience, other animal fibers such as alpaca, angora, llama, etc. will also felt. Some people have even felted with their dog's or cat's fur! Felting needles will also manipulate silk, flax, and hemp fibers and even synthetic fibers such as polyester fiberfill. Some people like to use less-than-ideal fibers on the inside of a sculpture if they happen to have other fibers on hand. Trial and error is your best bet if you want to experiment with other types of fiber.

SAFETY CONSIDERATIONS

Accidental pokes are definitely one drawback to needle felting. With more practice, and if you stay focused, ideally you can learn to minimize these. If you find that you are prone to poking yourself, it is best to take the precaution of wearing finger guards. When making 2-D pictures or small parts for sculptures, some people also use a tool such as tweezers or chopsticks, rather than their fingers, to hold wool in place.

Needle storage can also be a safety concern. Because felting needles are so sharp, I recommend always keeping them in a tube or tin. It is best not to leave them lying around where they could lead to accidental pokes, especially if you have pets or small children in the house! Several storage options are shown on page 26.

ETHICAL CONSIDERATIONS

Some people like to know if the wool they are using is from humanely raised sheep and is mulesing-free. Mulesing is a practice that is most common on large merino farms in Australia, where skin is removed from the buttocks of a lamb in order to prevent a life-threatening parasitic infection called flystrike. Tail docking, or shortening of the tail, is also a common practice. Mulesing is not as common in

other parts of the world as it is in Australia, and it is not commonly practiced in the US. The need for it depends a lot on the breed of sheep and the types of pests present in the landscape. If you are bothered by the idea of mulesing, there are now some wool certifications that help ensure the ethical treatment of sheep. Keep in mind that not all wool producers and sellers can afford to invest in these certifications, even if their practices are ethical and humane. In terms of shearing, sheep have been bred to produce a thick coat of hair fiber, and most of them do not mind being shorn! It is like getting a haircut and helps them stay cooler in the summer heat. I feel good about using sheep's wool, which is a wonderful, natural product. I know several shepherds personally, and they take great pride in the way that they raise and care for their animals. If this is a concern for you, look for wool that has a mulesing-free certification—or, better yet, purchase from small farms where you can talk to farmers directly about how they raise their sheep.

ARE THE DYES USED ON WOOL ECO-FRIENDLY?

In general, animal fibers such as wool take up dye easier than plant fibers such as cotton and linen and synthetic fibers such as acrylic, polyester, and nylon. Therefore, the dyes are fairly safe to use and to handle. The dyes used to dye wool are similar to any commercial dyes used to dye textiles for clothing or home decor applications. If you feel strongly about wanting to make sure the wool you are using is low-impact, you might look into getting plant-dyed wool or wool with an Oeko-Tex certification. It is also fun to learn to dye wool yourself!

GENERAL TIPS AND TECHNIQUES

- When you're sculpting, stab far into the center with the needle when you're creating a shape. Once the shape starts to firm up, stab less hard, closer to the surface.
- When you're making flat pictures, there is no need to stab in far with the needle. Be sure you are stabbing through the wool and backing fabric into the mat, but that usually means that only about ¼ inch (6 mm) or so of the tip of the needle should be poking down into the mat.
- Whenever you are ready to finish a piece and want to work on surface finishing, stab in gently with shallow pokes close to the surface and keep your pokes very close together. You will always see puncture holes, but this makes them less noticeable.
- You can't really stab too much. Keep stabbing until the wool is condensed down and smoothed out (not fuzzy-looking). When in doubt, stab more!
- Keep the needle going straight in and straight out. Avoid putting too much sideways pressure on the tip of the needle, since this can cause it to bend or break.
- Be careful of your other fingers, especially those you are using to hold wool in place while you stab it. If you find that you are prone to poking yourself, invest in finger guards or a protective glove or hold the wool in place with something other than your fingers.

THE Projects

All of the following projects are meant to be doable for beginners but still fun for more-seasoned felters. Some are a little harder and some a little easier, but if you're ready to jump right in, then start with whatever calls to you most. Some people like to felt for the season they're in, and others prefer to work ahead to give themselves more time to complete decorations well before a holiday is upon them. There are three projects per season. I hope they are as gratifying to make as they are for you to display in your home.

SPRING

Decorated Eggs

Decorating real eggs around Easter was a part of my childhood. Sometimes we would gather with my aunts and cousins to soak hard-boiled eggs in food dye and then draw on the eggs with colored pencils. One year, we started to make hollow eggs by draining out the insides. I had an egg stencil kit that I used to make flowers and designs on the hollow eggs with little markers. When my girls were young, I decorated wooden eggs with a wood burner and liquid watercolors. I hope you enjoy learning to make needle-felted eggs to celebrate the coming of spring! Unlike real eggs, they are soft and durable and can be enjoyed year after year.

Make each egg in the same way, using different coordinating colors to wrap each egg.

SUPPLIES

- 1 oz. core wool batting
- ⅛ oz. wool batting in the following colors: pink, coral, yellow, blue green, blue, purple, and cream
- 38 Triangle felting needles
- a mat to use as a work surface
- small scale (optional)

Decorated Eggs

Prepare your core wool.

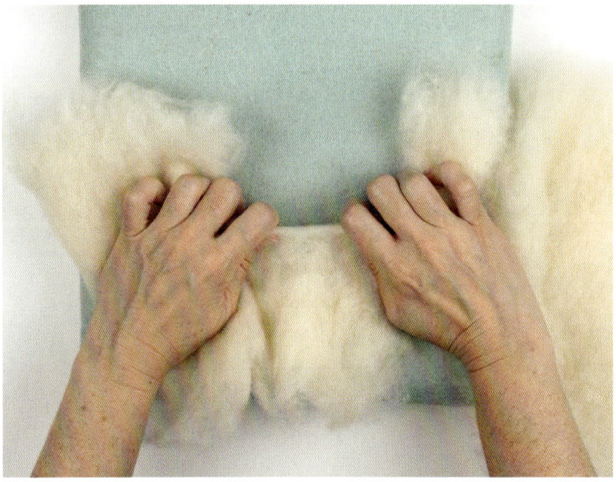

1. **Unfold your 1 oz. of core wool and tear it into six even strips.** If it is rectangular, start by tearing it in half lengthwise and then tear both halves into three pieces. Check that they are a similar size by weighing them on a small scale, if you have one. Move wool around if needed to make them as even as you can.

2. **Inspect your strips.** They should look similar to this. If your wool was thicker, they will be fairly small. If your wool was thinner, they may be longer and wider. It is the amount that is important by weight, since you can work with the wool as you roll it to make the strips narrower or wider if needed.

Make the egg shapes.

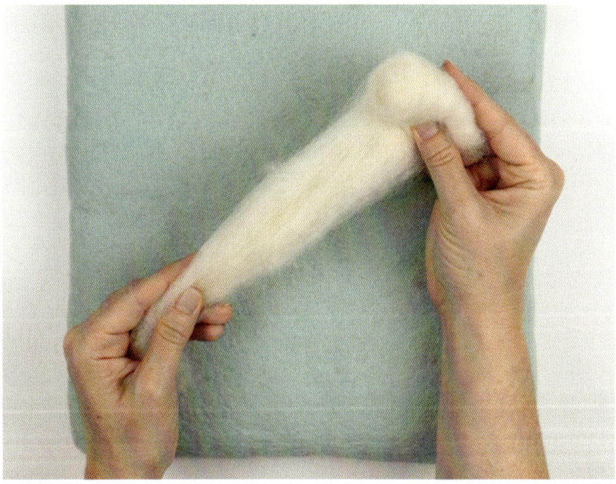

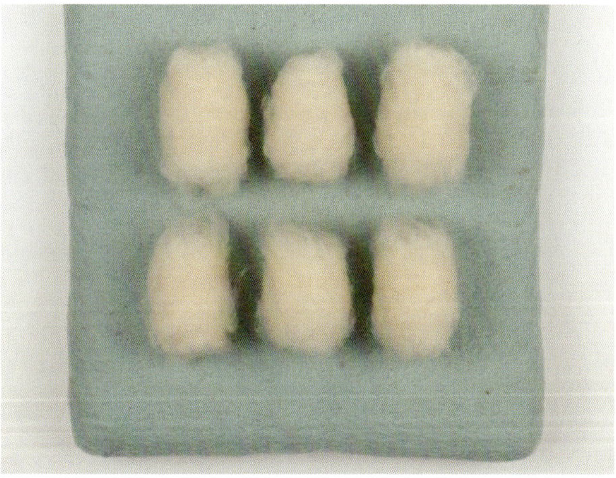

3. **Roll up each strip into an egg shape.** Pinch the wool together as you start the roll to concentrate more of it in the middle of the shape. Take care to keep more wool around the middle of the egg and not let the roll get too tall and narrow. It may help to stretch out the strip and make it narrower as you roll.

4. **Make sure that your rolls look similar before you start shaping the eggs.** Unroll the wool and redo if needed. The eggs should feel firm, but with a little give to them, when you squeeze them. If they are not rolled tightly enough, the shaping process will be longer and more difficult.

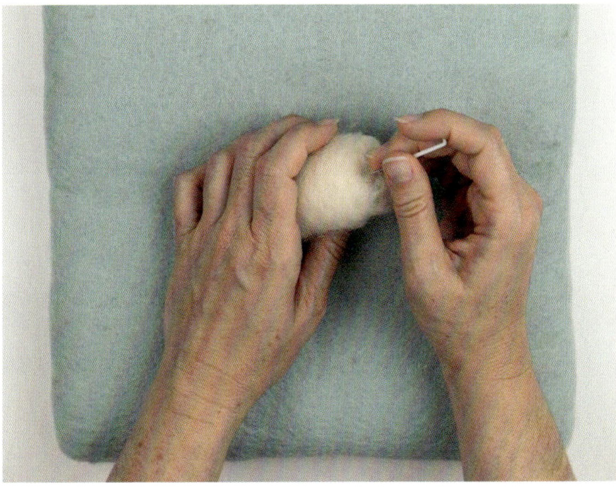

5. **To shape the egg, place it on the mat and start stabbing into it from the ends.** Make sure you are stabbing deep into the center of the egg in the early stages of felting it. Move gradually over the whole egg. Work mostly from the ends toward the middle, since this will help the egg stay round.

6. **Continue shaping.** You may want to compare it to a real egg while you are shaping, as a reference. Wherever you poke more, the wool will firm up and condense there. Turn the egg often while you are shaping so that you don't indent any one area too much. Make your stabs farther apart while you are establishing the shape.

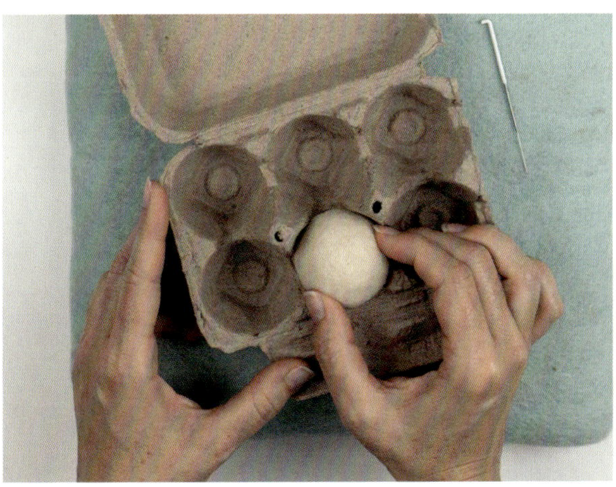

7. **Even out the surface.** Once you are happy with the shape of the egg and are ready to smooth the surface, make your stabs shallower and closer together. Stab more on any areas that are puffy or bumped out. Stab less on any indented areas, to even out the surface. You may want to use an egg carton to check your shaping.

Cover the eggs with color.

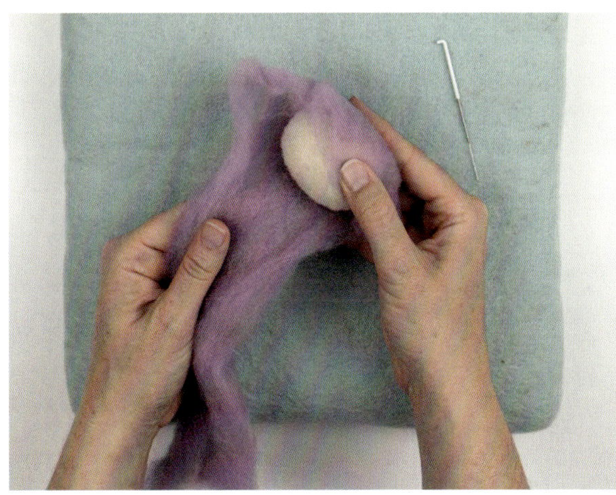

8. **Wrap the egg in dyed wool in a color you like,** overlapping the ends slightly and tearing off any extra. The wool should be thick enough that you can't see the core wool of the egg through the dyed wool. For good coverage, use more than one layer if your wool is too thin.

9. Start poking the dyed wool until it is well attached to the egg and smoothed out. Poke now with shallower stabs, going in far enough that the wool gets attached but not so far that you are altering the shape you created. Stabbing with pokes close together and at an even depth helps smooth the surface.

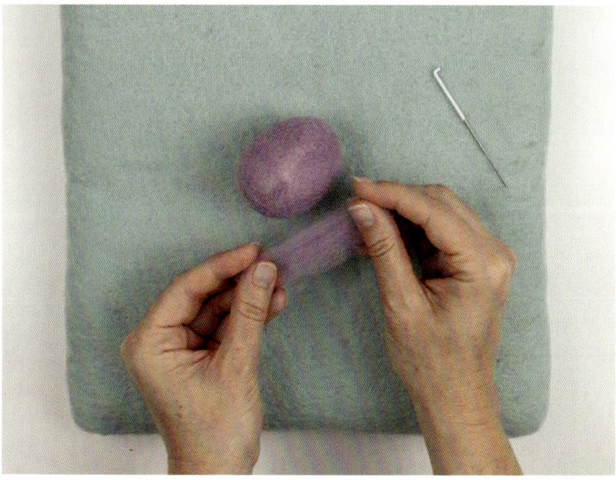

10. Once the dyed wool is well attached and smoothed out, **check for any areas where the cream core wool is still showing through.** Add extra pieces of dyed wool if needed to cover those areas. When adding wool, spread out the edges and it will not be noticeable.

Put on the leaf-and-dot design.

11. To start decorating the egg, tear off a thin strip of cream wool. It is a little easier to have one long strip run all the way around the egg, but if that doesn't work out, you can overlap smaller strips.

12. Stretch out the strip of wool and hold it on the egg. Go around the middle of the egg from top to bottom until the strip overlaps back where you started. Poke on the cream wool until it is well attached. Tidy the edges by pulling wool into place with the tip of the needle and poking in at an angle on the edges of the line.

TIP

If at any point you decide you don't like the wool you just put on and want to try again, simply pull it back up! Needle felting is very forgiving in this way. This will work whenever you are decorating a shape or making a flat picture.

13. **Tear a second strip of wool and wrap it around the egg,** dividing it into four even sections. Add extra pieces of wool to fill in any thin spots on these lines, making them an even width as they wrap around the egg.

14. **To make the leaf design on each line, first pull off small pieces of wool.** Most people tend to use too much wool. If your leaves are too big, simply tear them in half or start again with a smaller piece of wool.

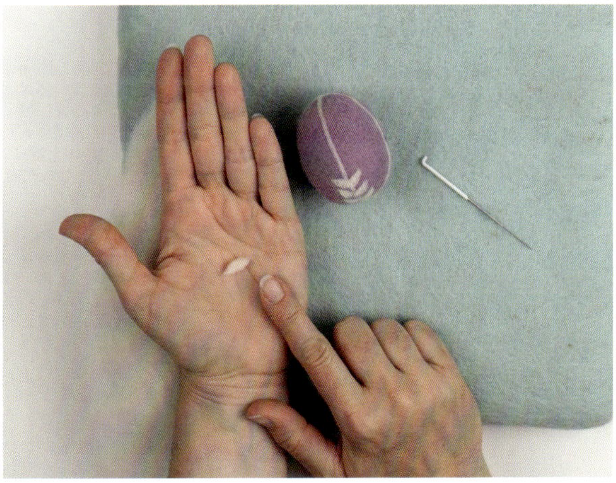

15. **Roll the wool back and forth on your palm with your pointer finger until it forms a leaf shape,** with a slightly rounded middle and pointy ends. It does this naturally when you roll it back and forth. Keeping your hands slightly moist with a little water from a sponge or wet washcloth makes it easier to form the leaves.

Decorated Eggs

16. Stab on each leaf, starting on the line. Use your needle to gently pull the wool into a point on both sides as you attach it. Put on the leaves in pairs, angling them diagonally so that they are pointing up slightly toward the top of the egg. See if you can fit between eight and ten pairs of leaves on each of the four lines.

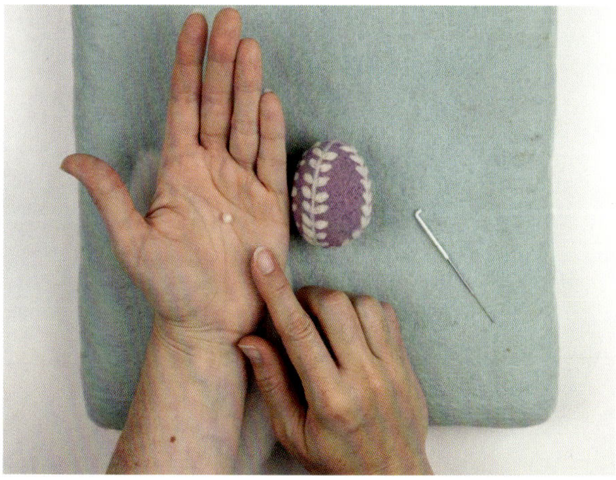

17. Make little balls to create a line of round dots in between the lines of leaves. Tear off very tiny bits of wool and roll these around on your palm to form the little balls. Each line should have five balls. Vary the sizes a bit.

18. Stab the balls on, putting the largest in the middle, then two that are slightly smaller next to that one, and then add the two smallest on the ends. If they are all about the same size, though, it will still look good! Stab into the edges of the balls. Because they are so small, they attach with only a few strategic stabs.

Outsunny

Carrot Garland

A garland can make any spot a little extra special. Perhaps they were once used only for special occasions, but you can put up a garland anywhere, anytime, and leave it up as long as you want!

Little puffy hearts were the first shape I ever needle felted. These quickly got turned into heart garlands. Felt garlands have become popular in recent years and can be made with any theme in mind, from animals to cacti. Being a local foodie, I enjoy a weekly trip to the farmers' market to pick up fresh veggies. This carrot garland was inspired by the spring market, when lettuce, turnips, radishes, and carrots fill up my market basket.

Use the pattern template to help with the size and shaping of the parts. You will need to make five carrots, five large leaves, five small leaves, and eight balls.

SUPPLIES

- 1 oz. core wool batting
- ½ oz. orange wool batting
- ⅛ oz. green wool batting
- 38 Triangle felting needles
- size 18 tapestry needle
- approx. 9 ft. of jute twine
- pattern template (see page 154)
- a mat to use as a work surface

Carrot Garland

Prepare the carrot shapes.

1. Divide the orange wool into five equal parts. Try to make rectangles that are approximately 4 by 6 inches (10.2 by 15.2 cm), but it is okay if they are not exactly the same.

2. Fold each piece into a carrot shape. Lay a rectangle of wool on the mat and start folding it up from one end, keeping the wool snug as you go. About halfway up the piece of wool, start folding more diagonally to make a pointed tip at the bottom and a wider top.

3. Roll up all your carrots before you start felting, to make sure they are similar to each other. Reroll or move wool from one to another if needed to even them up. If any end up too tall, tear off some wool at the top and add this to the shape in the middle or near the top to give more bulk where the carrot needs to be wider.

Felt the carrots.

4. Start felting the carrot by poking deeply into the wool. Poke first from each end to keep the carrot shorter, with the angle of the needle pushing wool toward the center. Once you have poked from each end and the carrot shape is holding together, then you can poke more on the middle of the carrot.

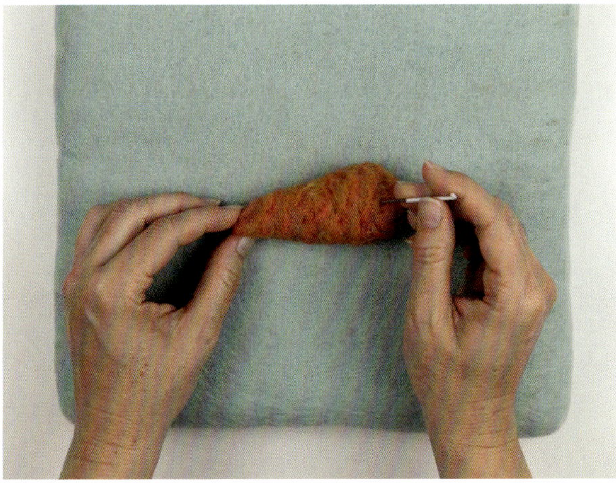

5. Continue stabbing in deep to establish the shape and make sure the carrot is firm on the inside. The needle should be penetrating to the middle of the carrot, sometimes even hitting the mat on the backside. Seeing deep puncture holes at this point means you are doing a good job!

6. Check your sizing and shaping periodically with the pattern template. If the carrot is still too big, keep stabbing it more. The more you stab, the more it will shrink down and get more firm. Once it is the right size, start working on smoothing the surface by poking in less deeply, with your pokes closer together.

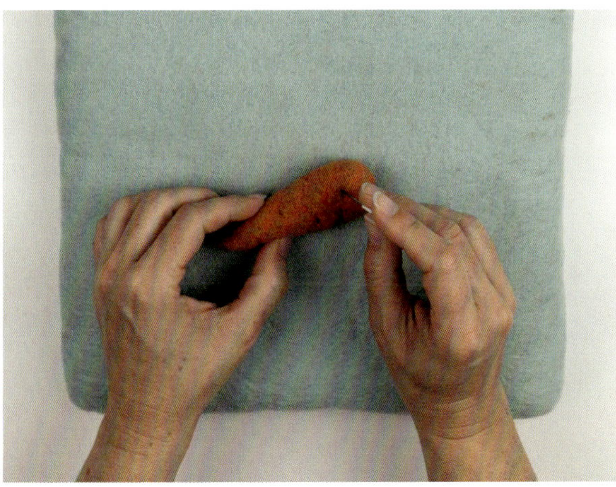

7. Once the carrot is firm with a smooth-looking surface, add some indents. Stab back and forth in a short line (about ¼ inch, or 6 mm) until you see an indent form. Then move on to make another one. These should be spaced randomly, staggering them an inch or 2 apart, all around the carrot.

Tear and fold the leaf wool.

8. To make the leaves, **tear thin strips of wool that are about twice as long as you want each leaf to end up.** Fold these in half, putting the ends together. The folded part will become the top of each leaf. Tear for all the leaves before you start felting them, to make sure you have enough wool. Use the pattern template as a guide.

Felt the leaves.

9. **Start each leaf by stabbing its edges,** angling the needle into the sides of the leaf and down into the mat. Once the shape is established and stuck to the mat, stab through the rest of the leaf except for the bottom. Leave a ¼- to-½-inch (6 to 13 mm) "tail" unfelted; this will be used to attach the leaf to the carrot.

10. After you have stabbed enough that the leaf will hold its shape, **carefully pull it up off the mat and turn it over.** Repeat the process on the back. Pull any wool that is sticking up at the edges toward the middle of the leaf with the tip of the needle and gently poke it down. Use the pattern template to check the shape.

11. **Continue felting the leaf on both sides until it is firm.** Then stab gently to smooth the surface, taking care at this point not to poke through the leaf into the mat, since this will push fibers to the other side and keep it fuzzy. Finally, stab in a line, moving back and forth down the center of the leaf to finish it.

12. **Make the remaining leaves using the same method.** The smaller leaves will naturally turn out more petite when you start with smaller pieces of wool. Each carrot will use one big and one small leaf. To attach the leaves, start with a big leaf and open up its unfelted "tail."

13. **Place the opened "tail" fibers on the top of the carrot.** Stab in deeply on these along with the very bottom of the felted part of the leaf, until the leaf is well attached and standing up on the carrot top. Then add the second, smaller leaf in the same way, a little to the side and slightly in front of the big leaf.

Tear and roll your core wool into ball shapes.

14. **To make the balls, tear 1 oz. of core wool into eight strips**. Depending on the thickness of the wool, they may be a little wider or narrower than what is shown here. Try to make your strips about 2½ inches (6.4 cm) wide and approximately 10 inches (25.4 cm) long. There may be some wool left over, which is okay.

15. To make a ball shape, **tear the strip in half** so that now you have two strips that are approximately 2½ by 5 inches (6.4 by 12.7 cm). Pinch the wool together and start rolling it toward you. Keep the strip narrow by squeezing it together or stretching it out so that the ball doesn't grow too wide.

16. Once you have used the first half of the strip, **turn the ball sideways (45 degrees)** and start wrapping the other half of the strip around it. It makes the finished felt stronger to have fibers overlapped in two different directions.

Carrot Garland

Felt the balls.

17. **Start poking into the ball.** It is okay if it does not start out very round. Stab in deeply first on any parts that are popped out to begin to establish a sphere. Poke less on any indented parts. Make sure you are stabbing all the way into the center of the ball when you are starting the shape. Stab five to ten times on a section and then turn.

18. **Continue turning it often so that you shape gradually,** always working to make it more and more round by where you stab with the needle. As you stab, it will start getting firmer and shrink down slightly in size. Use the pattern template as a guide for shaping and size.

19. Once the ball is round, **switch to stabbing in more gently,** going in about ¼ inch (6 mm) with the tip of the needle, and make your stabs closer together. This combo will help smooth the surface. When finished, the ball should still have enough give so that it can pass over the tapestry needle when you are constructing the garland.

Put it all together.

20. **Thread the twine onto the tapestry needle,** leaving a small tail. String all the parts of the garland, starting with two balls, then a carrot, then a ball, etc., until you get to the other end and finish with two balls. It can be a little hard to pull the pieces over the needle, but if they are not too firm, it will work!

Spring Tulips

One of my daughters loved to purchase a fresh flower bouquet every week to display on our table. I've gotten out of that habit, but because of my needle felting I am surrounded by different types of felted flowers. This tulip project illustrates how you can fill in a drawing with wool. I like to call this "coloring with wool" because it is similar to filling in a picture in a coloring book or doing a paint-by-number. Any number of line drawings including patterns meant for embroidery and other fiber arts can be adapted and used for needle felting.

SUPPLIES

- linen fabric, approximately 12 inches (30.5 cm) square
- white muslin fabric, approximately 9 inches (22.9 cm) square
- ⅛ oz. pieces of wool batting in the following colors: medium purple, dark purple, blue green, lime green, olive green, and cream
- 7-inch embroidery hoop
- 38 Star felting needles
- pattern template (see page 155)
- a mat to use as a work surface
- a thin permanent marker or other transfer method
- hot glue and glue gun or other craft glue
- a pair of sharp scissors

Spring Tulips

Transfer the pattern.

1. One method for getting the tulip pattern onto your fabric is to **tape the printed pattern on a window and then tape the linen fabric over it.** With those secured, carefully draw each line with a thin permanent marker. If you have other preferred pattern transfer methods, any of those can be substituted.

Fill in the picture.

2. **Place the pattern onto the mat.** It is ideal if the whole project will fit. If not, do one section at a time and then pull up the project and put it on a different section of the mat to continue. Start with dark-purple wool and tear off thin, small pieces that are slightly larger than the areas you will be filling in.

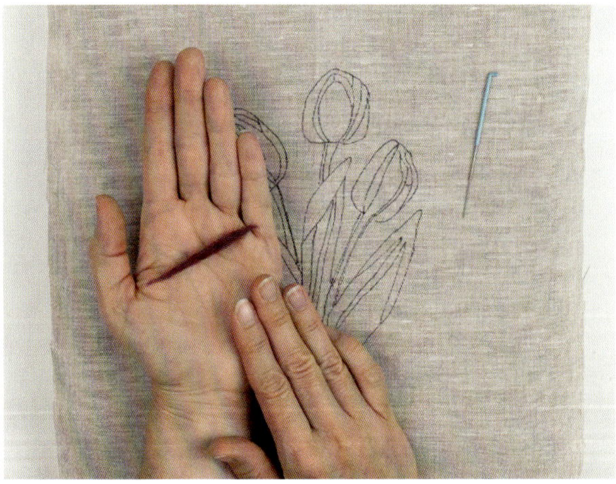

3. **Smooth the wool strips.** When using thin strips of wool, it is helpful to condense and smooth the wool by rolling it back and forth on your palm, similar to making a "snake" with clay. Alternately, you can roll the wool between your fingers. Keeping your hands slightly moist by using a damp washcloth or sponge can be helpful.

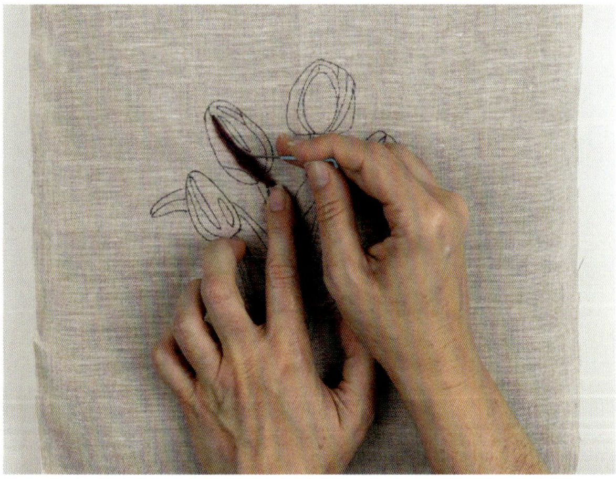

4. To fill in the picture, **place the wool where you want it and start stabbing it.** Stab through the wool and fabric down into the mat about ¼ inch (6 mm) until the wool is attached and flattened out. Hold the wool in place with your other hand as you continue to stab, being careful to keep fingers away from the sharp tip of the needle.

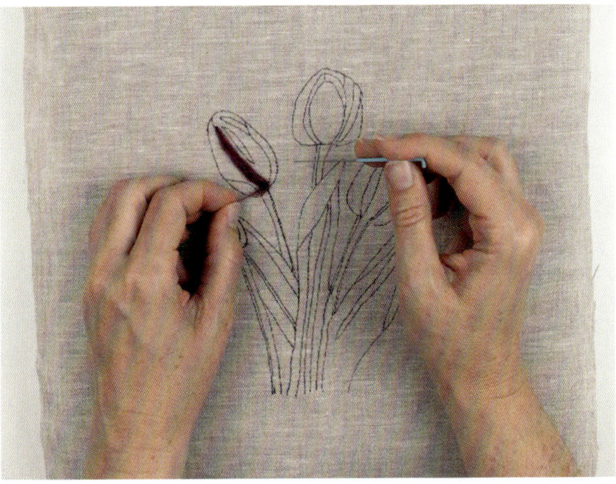

5. **Remove extra material.** If you get to the end of the area you are filling in and there is extra wool, pinch near where you want it to end, tear off the extra bit, and then continue to poke on the end until it doesn't show. Alternatively, you can fold the extra "tail" back up on itself and poke it down.

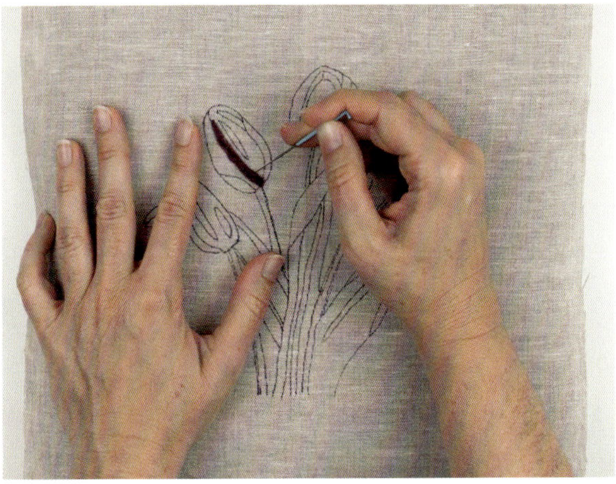

6. **Clean up the edges.** It will help make a smooth, tidy edge if you stab in at an angle rather than straight up and down. You can also gently pull wool into place with the tip of the needle and then poke it down. It is still good to stab straight in when poking the middle of a section of color.

TIP

To get a uniform, smooth surface look, try to apply the wool so that you end up with an even thickness across the whole picture. On many of the areas of color, you will need to use multiple layers to achieve this. When adding another layer, try to keep the wool fibers going in the same direction as the layer below. You will start to be able to tell which direction the fibers are going as you gain more experience with the wool fiber. As with any design, you can take wool off and try again until you are happy with the result.

7. Once the smaller, thinner sections of color are filled in on a tulip, **use slightly larger pieces of light purple to fill in all around them.**

8. **Finish the tulip.** Each area of color (especially the larger ones) should be covered by an initial piece of wool, then small pieces or little rolls to fill in thin spots, particularly at the edges, and then one final piece over the top of all the layers to give a smooth, uniform finish.

9. **Tear long, thin strips of wool to use for the stems.** Roll these on your palm to condense the wool and help it hold together, as described in step 3. If this proves difficult, you can use shorter strips of wool and overlap them. Stems may still need two to three layers depending on how thick your strips are.

10. **Remove extra material.** When using long strips of wool, you may have extra at the end. Use one of the methods in step 5 to deal with this extra wool; either tear off the end or fold it back up on itself and poke it down.

11. **Use larger pieces of wool when filling in larger areas.** Try to tear them so that they are a similar size and shape as the area you need to fill in. If there are any spots that are not well covered with wool, you can still fill those in with extra pieces that are smaller.

12. **Continue using the same techniques until the whole picture is filled in.** Stab each area until the wool is completely flattened out. Keeping your stabs very close together and at an even depth will help give a smooth surface finish.

Pull up the picture and put on finishing touches.

13. **One you feel happy with the piece, pull it off the mat.** This can take some tugging. Proceed slowly, but don't worry too much—it will be okay!

14. With the picture off the mat, **look for areas where the fabric is not well covered** or the wool is still fuzzy and not well attached. Also, look at the back, because if there is not much wool coming through on the backside, there is not enough wool on the front. Add more wool layers and do more stabbing if needed.

Frame the picture in a hoop.

15. **Put the picture into the hoop, with the white muslin fabric behind the design.** Follow this order: Place the inner hoop, then white fabric, then tulip picture, then outer hoop. The white fabric keeps the linen from being see-through and finishes the backside.

16. **Pull the fabric tight.** Make sure you like the position of the picture in the hoop before you fully tighten the screw. It can take a few tries to get it just where you want it.

17. **Cut off the extra fabric,** leaving about 1 inch (2.5 cm) to glue to the hoop. Other finishing methods for hoops can be used instead, but I find this one to be quick, easy, and effective.

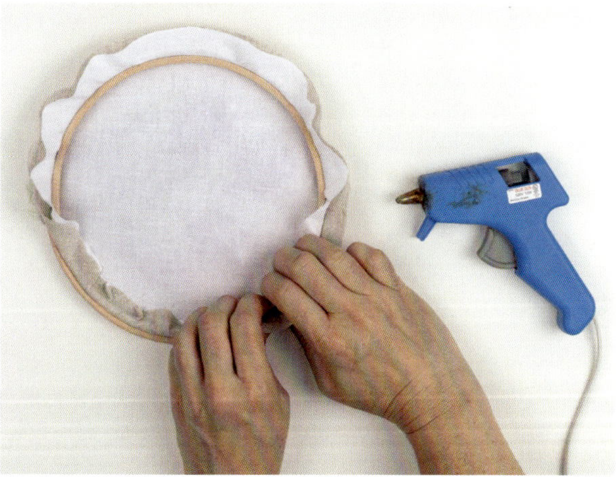

18. **Attach the fabric to the hoop;** I use hot glue, but another glue could be substituted. Place a small bead of glue on the hoop itself and then fold the fabric over tightly onto it. Do the white fabric first and then go back around to glue the linen fabric over that. It works best to glue 2 to 3 inches (5.1 to 7.6 cm) at a time.

SUMMER

Moonstone Succulent

I have always loved seeing real potted plants in other people's homes and commercial buildings. Unfortunately, I am not very good at tending live plants myself, and if they live, mine usually look a bit scraggly and overwatered (or the opposite—who can tell?!). Unfortunately, I am not a fan of fake plants, no matter how real they look. That's just me; I know that plenty of people like to decorate with faux decor, but I am unapologetically drawn to what is real and natural. Somehow, I still like felted plants. Perhaps it is because they are made with a natural material and not mass-produced. So, when I first started making needle-felted succulents, it seemed like a great compromise. They are really cute, don't need to be watered, and always look their best!

The first image of this project shows three of the following succulent plants grouped together in a larger pot. If you prefer that look, simply gather enough wool and make more plants.

SUPPLIES

- ⅛ oz. of wool batting in the following colors: sage green, coral, and dark brown
- 42 Triangle and 38 Triangle felting needles
- a small plant pot
- pattern template (see page 156)
- a mat to use as a work surface

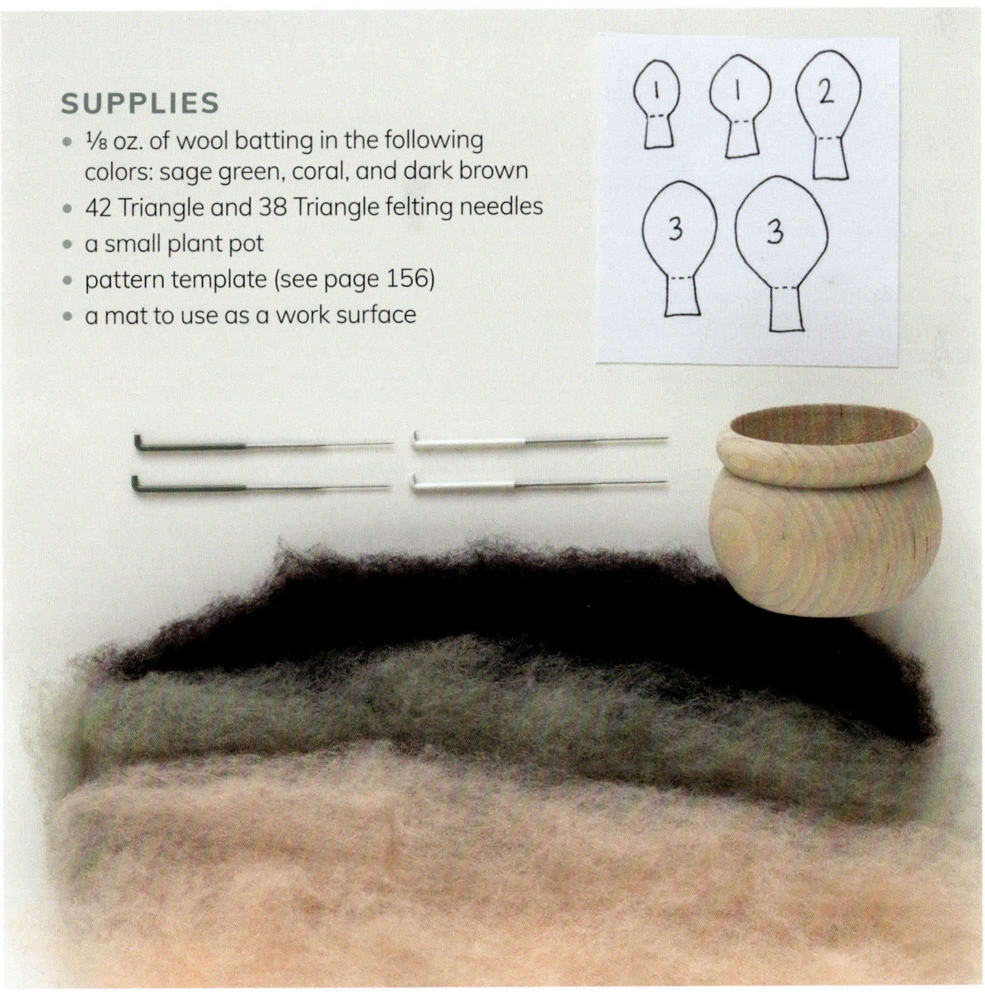

Moonstone Succulent

Prepare the wool.

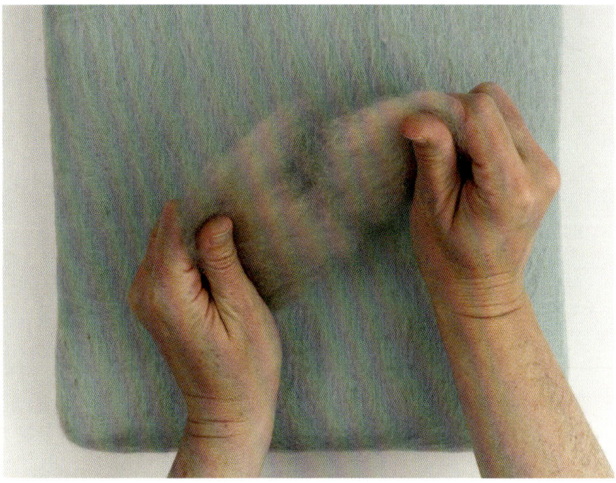

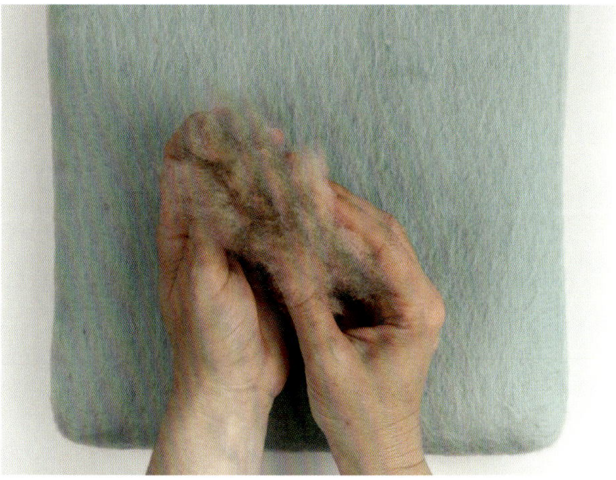

1. Mix the two colors together, using hand blending. Tear each color into three equal pieces. Blend one of each at a time and then move on to the next pieces until all the wool is blended. To start, hold two pieces of wool, one on top of the other, in your left hand. Tear the wool in half, pulling some of both colors into your right hand.

2. Stack the wool you pulled off back on top of the wool in your left hand. Keep the fibers aligned in the same direction as you continue to pull off wool with your right hand, then stack it back on top of the wool in your left hand. Stop blending when the colors are heathered together, but you can still recognize each one.

Make the leaves.

3. Pull apart the blended wool into the amounts you will need for the leaves. Use the pattern template to see how many leaves to make in each size. Try to use up all the wool that you blended for the leaves to end up the correct sizes. Shape the leaves with the 42 Triangle needle. Put them together with the 38 Triangle.

4. To shape the leaves, first **take one of your pieces of blended wool and fold it down.** The rounded top part will become the puffy leaf. Do not felt the bottom part of the leaf. Instead, leave an unfelted "tail" about ¼ inch (6 mm) to ½ inch (12 mm) long. It will be used to help hold the leaf during shaping, and when you connect the leaves at the end.

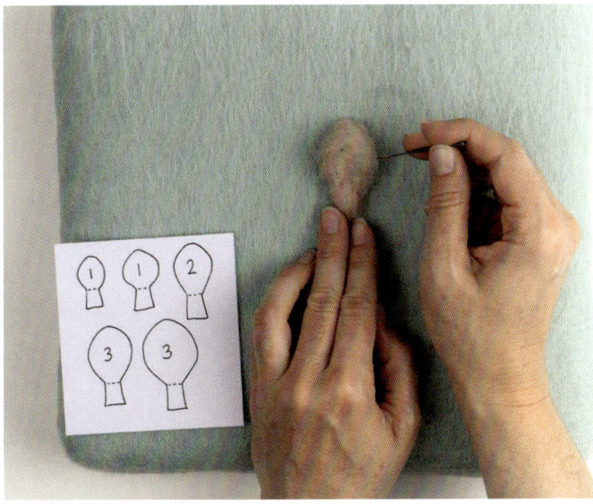

5. **Stab in at an angle, poking the outside edge of the leaf.** Stab through the wool down into the mat. It is okay if the leaf gets a little stuck to the mat. This helps establish the shape. Once you have stabbed around the outer edge, then stab straight down into the leaf about 10 times to get the wool to hold together.

6. Don't spend too long on the front side before you **carefully pull the leaf up and flip it over to the backside.** Use the needle to fold any fuzzy fibers at the edges in toward the middle and poke them down. Continue shaping the leaf from the backside by stabbing in from the sides, as well as on the middle.

7. **Continue shaping gradually, turning the leaf from front to back.** Poke harder through the leaf to establish the shape but then switch to gentle stabs to smooth the surface. Stab in only about ¼ inch (6 mm) with the tip of the needle at this point, with your pokes close together. Use the template as a guide and stop when the leaf is firm.

Put the plant together.

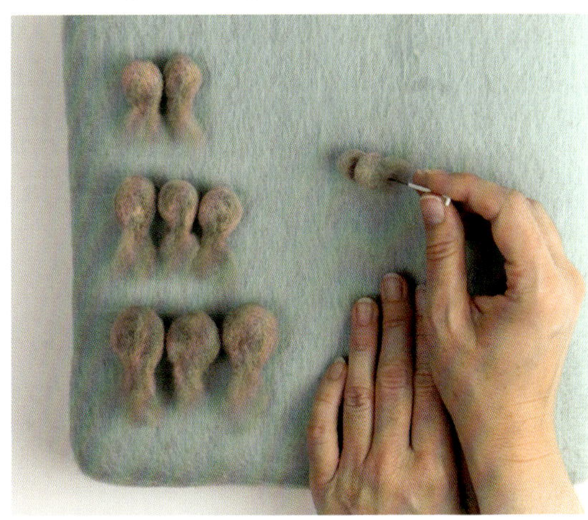

8. **Make all the leaves in the same way.** The amount of wool determines their size. To put the succulent together, first start with the two smallest leaves. Hold them together on the mat and stab in hard through the unfelted "tails" at the bottom of the leaves until they hold together.

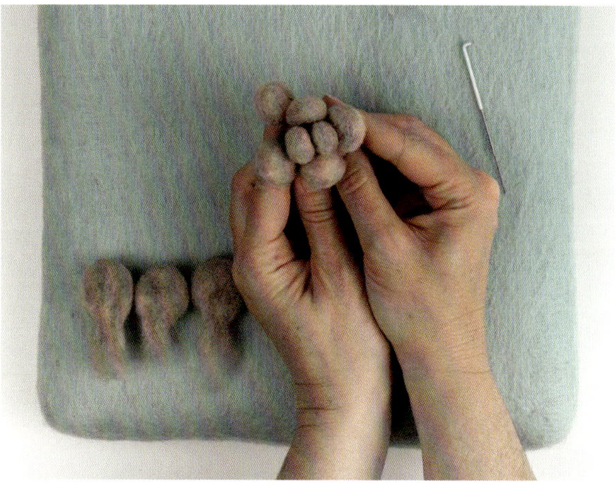

9. **Continue putting on leaves, smallest to largest, working from the middle outward.** Sometimes it helps to think of them going on in pairs, across from each other. Hold the leaves together and take a look at the placement before you stab on each new one. You can pull any of the leaves off and try again if needed.

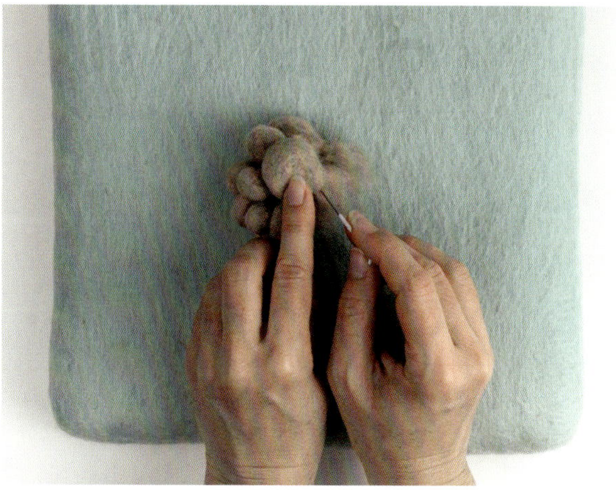

10. **Keep going until all the leaves are attached together,** with the largest on the outside of the plant.

Place the plant in its pot.

11. With the plant finished, **wrap the dark-brown wool around the bottom** and then stuff this bundle of wool and plant into the pot.

12. If the plant isn't secure in the wool or the wool is too puffy and sticking up, **poke down into the wool to flatten it out.** To get the brown wool and plant to hold together better, poke in from the sides to catch some of the brown wool near the plant and attach them together.

Beach View

In all of needle felting, making landscapes is the thing that comes the most naturally to me. Perhaps this is because I love to spend time in nature, taking in beautiful views. As a busy business owner living in the Midwest, I don't get to see mountain vistas, sunny beaches, or desert rock formations as often as I would like. However, creating artwork that I can display around me that captures the essence and beauty of those places has become the next-best thing to being there. This beach project is a good introduction to making needle-felted scenes. I hope you enjoy creating it and are inspired to make other landscapes, such as places you've been or places you hope to visit someday.

SUPPLIES

- linen fabric, approximately 12 inches (30.5 cm) square
- ⅛ oz. pieces of wool batting in the following colors: pale blue and pale tan
- 1⁄16 oz. pieces of wool batting in the following colors: white, sage green and dark olive green
- ⅛ oz. pieces of roving in the following colors: dark turquoise, light turquoise, and light brown
- 7-inch embroidery hoop
- 38 Star felting needles
- a mat to use as a work surface
- hot glue and glue gun or other craft glue
- a sharp pair of scissors

Beach View

Add the sky.

1. **Center the linen fabric on your mat.** Then lay out the piece of pale-blue wool and pull off extra from the ends. Use the hoop to gauge its size; it should extend beyond the hoop about 1 inch (2.5 cm). Remove the hoop and start poking it with the needle, going down through the wool and fabric into the mat until the wool is flattened and attached to the fabric.

Start the water and sand.

2. **Lay out the roving for the water and sand.** Overlap the sky with the turquoise roving. Think of the picture in thirds: The sky should take up the top third, the water should take up the middle third, and the sand and dunes should take up the bottom third, approximately.

3. **Spend time stabbing all these colors until the wool is very flat and well attached to the fabric.** If it is still fuzzy or fluffy or has fibers that aren't clearly attached, continue stabbing. While I prefer the control of a single needle, using a tool for this step can help the project go faster.

4. Once the wool is flattened, if you see any thin spots where the fabric is showing through, **add extra pieces of wool to fill those in.** The fibers are aligned horizontally in the pieces of wool that are already attached. If you add any extra pieces, try to keep the fibers going in that same direction, because this way they are less likely to show.

Add the clouds.

5. **Make clouds by adding a few wispy pieces of white wool.** Use the needle to pull the wool down into indents in the top of the clouds so that they have rounded parts at the top, similar to real clouds. Stab until they are attached, leaving the bottom of the clouds mostly straight and horizontal.

6. Take small wispy pieces of the light-turquoise roving (lighter water color) and **add these to the bottom of the clouds** to make them "pop" a bit and have more dimension.

TIP

When adding small details to wool paintings such as the clouds, waves, grass, and boat in this picture, use less wool than you think you need. When I am teaching classes, most beginners tend to use too much wool for these elements, which makes them more difficult to create. Occasionally I need to encourage a student to use more wool, but usually it is the opposite, and for small details less wool is almost always the way to go. It is easier to add more if you need to rather than trying to manipulate a piece of wool that is too big.

Finish the water.

7. Take some thin pieces of white wool, stretch them out, and **add them to the sky right above the waterline.** Make them thin enough that some of the blue sky still shows beneath these pieces. They are meant to look like haze in the distance.

8. **Finish the water** by laying out wispy pieces of the dark-turquoise wool on the light-turquoise wool. Keep the pieces horizontal and stagger them so they are a little random. Put a little more at the edges of the piece than you do in the middle of the water.

9. **Take pieces of light-turquoise wool** and lay them over the dark-turquoise part of the water. The idea is to blur the line where they meet. Add more of this color in the middle of the water than at the edges of the piece. Continue adding wool until you like the effect.

10. **Poke down all these thin pieces of wool.** It works best to stab one end into the fabric and then hold the wool in place with your other hand while you stab along the rest of the length of wool. Continue stabbing until all this extra wool is attached.

Make some waves.

11. Add some cresting waves with pieces of white wool. Roll the pieces back and forth on your palm to prepare them. Poke them on by catching the edges all the way around, leaving the middle of the waves slightly puffy. Make the crests smaller in the distance and larger at the shoreline.

Create sand dunes.

12. Lay out large pieces of sand-colored wool. These "sand dunes" should start out higher at the edge of the picture and curve down to where they overlap each other near the bottom of the picture. Fold under the top edge so that there is enough wool there to make a clean line. Use the hoop to check the placement.

13. Start attaching the sand dunes. Poke in at an angle along the edge, catching the backside where you folded the wool. Once the edge is tacked down, poke at an angle from the opposite direction toward the edge. After the edge is secure, continue poking the rest of the sand down, with your needle going straight in.

14. Add a wispy piece of sand color over top of the darker-brown roving. This makes it a little more interesting, with a less stark contrast.

Add the grass.

15. Spread some small pieces of dark-olive-green wool on top of the sand dunes and then poke them down. Make some of these pieces thin enough that some of the sand color shows through. Don't cover all the sand.

16. Pull off pieces of sage-green wool and roll them on your palm, as though you're making a snake. Tear off their thin ends to make some a little shorter than the others. When their lengths are varied, the grass will look random, like it does in nature. Make a lot of them.

17. Fold each "snake" in half and then place it on the sand, on an area of dark olive green. Poke the most at the bottom while holding the tops in place and angle your needle in from the sides. Don't poke the tips and don't flatten it all the way, so that it still looks wispy and a little 3-D.

18. As you are adding the rest of the grass, try to keep its placement slightly random, forming little clumps. Make sure that you vary the sizes that sit next to each other as you put them on. Having some smaller blades of grass here and there helps it look more realistic.

Make a tiny sailboat.

19. Once you have added as much grass as you want, it is time to **make the sailboat.** Use a tiny piece of dark olive green that you roll in between your fingers before poking it down. Make it about ½ inch (12.7 mm) long and give it a slight angle.

20. **Make the sails with two little pieces of white wool.** These should form triangles, with the one on the left being a little bigger than the one on the right. Roll these in between your fingers before you put them on, then gently pull the wool into place with the needle.

Pull up the picture and put on finishing touches.

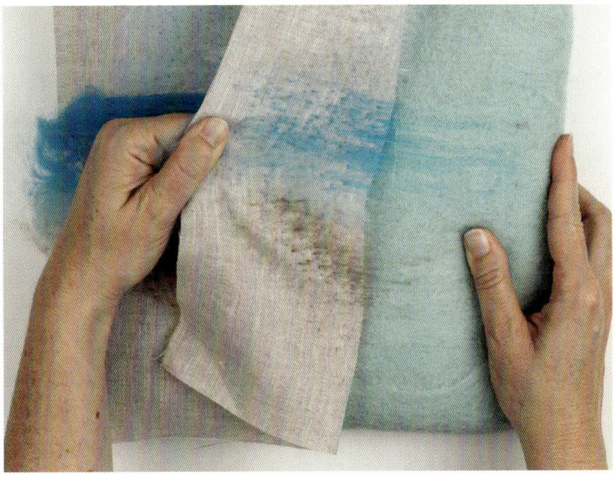

21. **Carefully pull the picture up off the mat.** This can take some tugging, but don't be afraid—the picture will be okay!

22. With the picture off the mat, **assess which areas are not as well felted or well attached and need more poking.** Go back over those areas. Also, now is the time to add more wool to any spots where you see fabric showing through.

Frame the picture in a hoop.

23. **When you are happy with the piece, put it into the hoop.** Pull the fabric tight and then tighten the screw as much as you can. It can take a few tries to get it right where you want it.

24. **Cut off the extra fabric,** leaving about 1 inch (2.5 cm) of fabric for gluing to the hoop. Make sure all of the wool is attached to this fabric on the edges, so that it will easily fold around the backside when you glue the fabric to the hoop and will not stick out afterward.

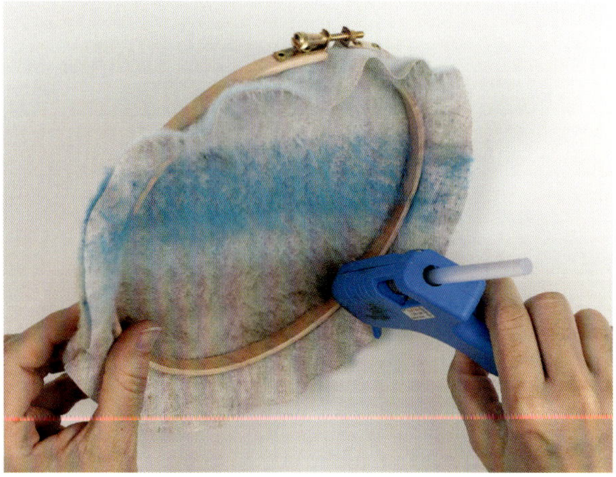

25. **Attach the fabric to the hoop;** I use hot glue, but another glue could be substituted. Place a small bead of glue on the hoop itself and then fold the fabric over tightly onto it. Do 2 to 3 inches (5.1 to 7.6 cm) at a time so that the glue doesn't set before you can get the fabric onto it.

26. **Continue to add glue** and fold the fabric around until you've secured all the fabric on the back side. Enjoy looking at and petting the fuzzy backside where all the wool poked through!

Citrus Coasters

My dad taught me to always use coasters. He loves to fill his drinks up with ice, and you don't want to end up with rings on a nice wooden table! This project utilizes a cookie (or biscuit) cutter, which is a great technique to have in your needle felting repertoire. In fact, it is perhaps the easiest way to make flat shapes, be they ornaments, leaves, flower petals, or, in this case, a perfectly round circle.

SUPPLIES

- 1 oz. core wool batting
- ⅛ oz. pieces of batting in the following colors: orange, bright orange, yellow, and lime green
- 3½-inch-round cookie cutter
- 38 Triangle felting needles
- pattern template (see page 156)
- a mat to use as a work surface

Citrus Coasters

Fill the cutter with core wool.

1. Divide 1 oz. of core wool into four equal parts. Use one part per coaster. Tear off pieces that are slightly larger than the cookie cutter and start filling it up. You will need three to four layers depending on how thick or thin your core wool is.

2. Try to keep the wool layers lying as flat as possible and vary the direction of the fibers in each layer. That will help make sturdier felt.

Begin felting the coaster.

3. Start poking down the core wool, stabbing in hard enough that your needle is going into the mat just slightly as you are stabbing through the wool. Poke the outside edge of the circle first, trying to keep the wool pushed outward so it is filling up the cookie cutter.

4. After you've poked the wool and it has started to condense down, **press your fingers around on the coaster** to check for spots that are thinner than others. Add smaller pieces of wool to those areas to even them out, and poke them down to attach them.

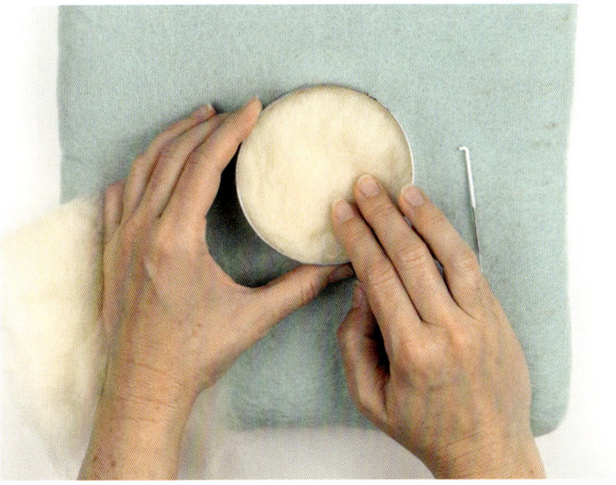

5. **Pull the coaster up off the mat, flip it over, and then put it back into the cookie cutter.** Poke now from the backside to continue to firm it up and condense the wool. Add extra pieces of wool to any thin spots you can feel on this side.

Finish the edges.

6. **Take the coaster out of the cookie cutter to work on the edges.** Take the leftover core wool and tear off pieces to wrap around the edges. Overlap four or five pieces until you've gone all the way around the coaster, putting this extra wool around the edges. If there is any core wool left, check one last time for thin spots.

TIP

Use up the entire ¼ oz. of core wool for each coaster. Once you have done the edges, if you have wool left over, add the rest to the coaster so that it will end up the same thickness as the others. If there are any thin areas, add it to those. If not, try to spread out the fibers of the leftover core wool and lay it out evenly over one side of the coaster so that it won't alter the work you have done.

Citrus Coasters

7. **Continue to work on the coaster,** especially the edges, by poking with the needle around the outside of the coaster. Then poke more on the top. Poke more on any places where it is thicker and more bumped out, and less on areas that are already thinner, working to keep it flat and uniform.

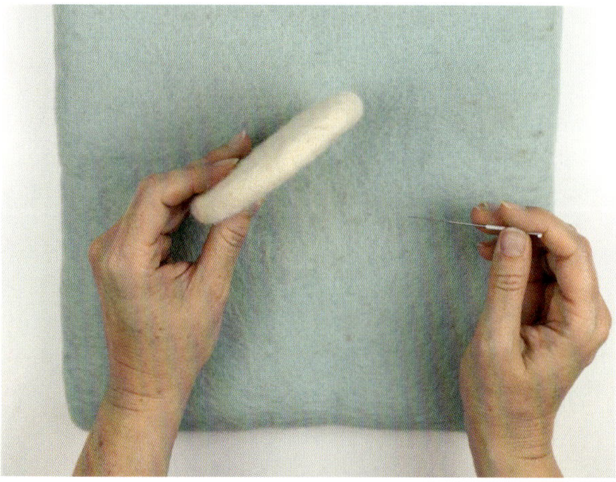

8. Before you start the colored edge, **make sure that the coaster is nice and firm and lies flat.** You can test it by putting a glass on it to see if it holds it well. When you're smoothing its surface, you do not need to keep going through all the wool layers and down into the mat. Poke more gently near the surface, with pokes close together.

Put on the outer ring of dyed wool.

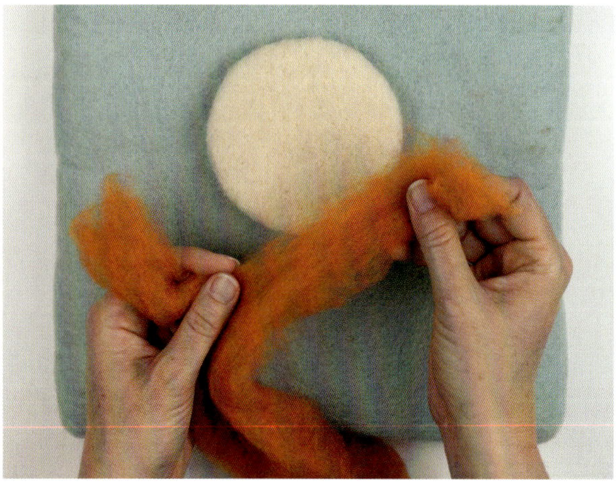

9. **Tear a strip of colored wool to use around the edge.** This will wrap around, creating a ring about ¼ inch (6 mm) on the top and bottom of the coaster. It is okay if you decide not to worry about the bottom as much, because it will not be seen.

10. **Gently pull the wool into place with the needle,** trying to keep the edge as rounded as possible on the top of the coaster. If needed, fill in around the edge with smaller pieces of wool.

11. Once the whole outside of the coaster is covered in colored wool, **work on poking it down until it is well attached,** smooth, and flat.

12. **Step back and take a look at your coaster.** It should look similar to this before you start the triangles.

Add the triangle segments (method 1).

13. **The first method for adding the triangles is to "eyeball" them.** Tear off six small pieces of wool, fold them into triangle shapes, and arrange them on the coaster. Start tacking them down gently at the edges, in case you need to pull them up and move them around.

14. When you're happy with the placement of the triangles, **finish poking them down** until they are also nice and flat and smoothed out on the coaster. Be sure to leave cream core wool showing around all sides of the triangles. The more even you can make the spacing, the better the triangles will look.

Add the triangle segments (method 2).

15. The alternate method for putting on the triangles is to **use the pattern template.** Hold it in place (you may want to use straight pins). Poke through the pattern repeatedly on the lines of the triangles. In the picture, I show how to poke on only one triangle, but it is best to do all of them at the same time for correct placement.

16. Pull up the pattern template. You should now be able to see the triangle lines enough to fill them in with colored wool.

17. Take small pieces of dyed wool and fill in the triangles, carefully pulling wool into place with the tip of the needle at the edges before you poke it down.

Finish it up.

18. Keep poking all over the coaster until it is nice and flat and very firm, so that it will hold glasses well without tipping them.

FALL

Mushrooms and Moss

I love to go walking in the woods. Living in Michigan, I am fortunate to have an abundance of parks and nature preserves nearby. While I'm walking, I love to stop and admire the many types of moss and fungi that cross my path. This project is inspired by the amazing variety of beautiful growing things that can be found in the forest, if you slow down and become observant enough to notice them. Displaying this little mushroom sculpture in my home feels like I'm bringing a little bit of the forest in with me.

SUPPLIES

- 1 oz. core wool batting
- ⅛ oz. pieces of wool batting in the following colors: camel brown, dark brown, and green
- 4-inch-round wool "foundation" (make a ¾-inch-thick [1.9 cm] coaster as a substitute if needed)
- 38 Triangle felting needles
- a mat to use as a work surface

Mushrooms and Moss

Prepare the mushroom caps.

1. **Tear roughly circular pieces of core wool to make the mushroom caps.** You will need two to three pieces of wool per cap, stacked on top of each other. These pieces should be about an inch larger than you want the caps to end up. Try for finished diameters of approximately 1¼, 1¾, and 2¼ inch (3.2, 4.4, and 5.7 cm).

2. **Take the stack of core wool and fold the outer edges down and under,** around to the backside, forming a puffy circle shape.

3. **Place the folded-under circle on the mat.** Start poking it in from the edges toward the center, at an angle, catching the layers on the backside and poking down into the mat. Then poke a little on the center of the cap, but not so much that it flattens.

4. **Pull it off the mat and turn it over to the other side.** Stab from the edges toward the middle again, flattening out this side more by stabbing all the way through the cap to firm it up. Then turn it over again. Poke from the sides toward the middle to keep it rounded. The wool will move in the direction you are stabbing.

Cover the caps with brown wool.

5. **Continue poking until the cap is fairly firm.** It should be round on the top but flatter on the bottom. Then make the other two caps so that you end up with one small, one medium, and one large.

6. All three of the mushroom caps will be finished in the same way. You will need to repeat steps 6-11 for each cap. First, **tear off a piece of camel-brown wool** to cover the cap.

7. **Fold under the long edge of the wool and wrap this folded edge around the bottom of the cap.** Hold it in place while you tear off the extra wool at the top. Alternately, you can stab all the way around the bottom edge first, so the wool stays in place, and then tear off the extra at the top.

8. **Start poking on the camel-brown wool until it is flattened and attached to the cap.** When you are working on the surface finishing, poke about ¼ inch (6 mm) down into the cap material with the tip of the needle. Make your stabs close together until the wool isn't fuzzy anymore and the cap is firm.

TIP

When working on mushroom caps where you don't want the top color to be visible on the other side, use shallower pokes. If the brown wool does poke through the bottom of the cap, finish smoothing the brown wool and add more core wool to the underside of the cap to cover up any bleed-through.

9. **Tidy up the bottom of the cap** by poking in between the core wool and the camel-brown wool, pulling any stray fibers into the indent between the colors. Then poke the brown wool more from the sides to finish the bottom edge and make sure it is well attached to the cap.

Embellish the cap.

10. For a final touch, **take a wispy piece of core wool and add it to one side of the cap.** Poke it gently until it is attached, with camel-brown wool showing through it.

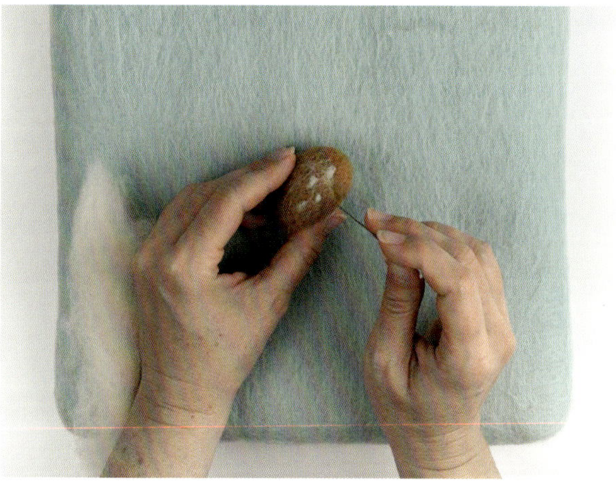

11. **Add some tiny dots of core wool on top of the wispy piece you just added.** You can do this by tearing off very small pieces and rolling these between your fingers to condense the wool. Then stab them gently to attach them. Keep them random sizes and shapes. You need only four to five dots.

Make the stems.

12. Tear three thin strips of core wool about 2, 2½, and 3 inches (5.1, 6.4, and 7.6 cm) wide. Roll each one up to make the stems. Keep the wool snug as you roll, so that they start out pretty firm even before you start stabbing them. The width of each strip will become the length of the stem.

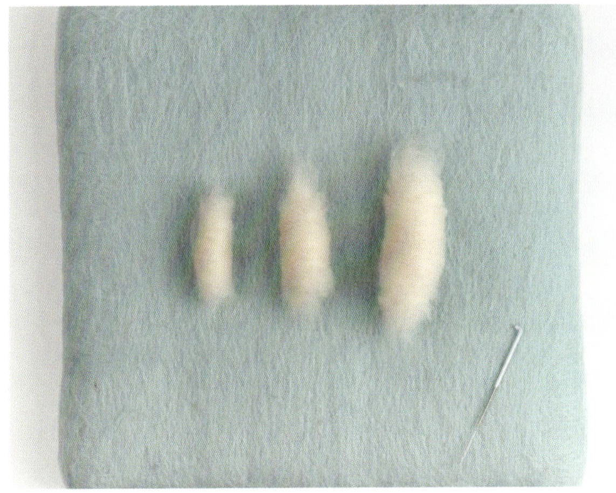

13. Make a small, medium, and large size to match the mushroom caps. Hold them together with each cap to test the sizing. If they are too large, try again, using less wool. It is common to make them too large rather than too small.

14. Poke up and down their length, turning them as you go. On the first pass, stab all the way into the middle of the stems, making sure you are making them firm so that they will stand straight. Then go around again, stabbing more gently to smooth the surface. Leave ½ inch (1.3 cm) of unstabbed space at the top and bottom.

15. Add a small, wispy piece of brown wool to one side of the stem. This makes it a little more interesting and realistic once it is paired with its cap.

Attach the stems to the caps.

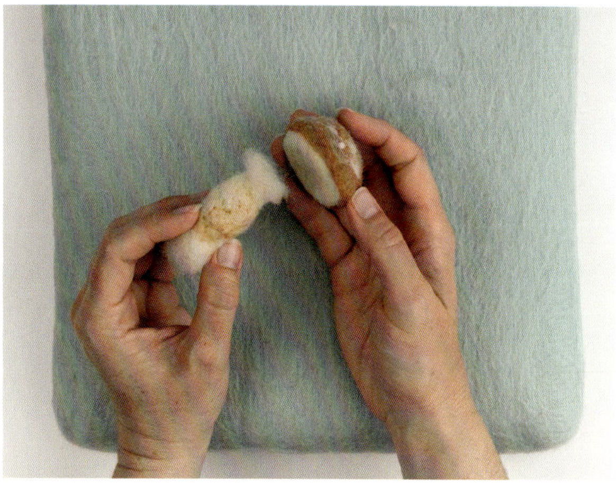

16. **Pull open the top-of-stem fibers** that you didn't poke when you were making it. Having these unfelted fibers opened up will help you easily attach the stem to the cap.

17. **Put the cap back on the mat and hold the stem on it** while you poke into the open fibers. Poke all the way around the top of the stem until it is attached to the cap. Don't poke so deep that you poke cream fibers all the way through the cap. If you do, you may want to cover those with more camel-brown wool.

Create a hill for the mushrooms.

18. Once you have finished all three mushrooms, **start building up the foundation.** Add multiple layers of core wool to one side of your wool foundation or coaster to make it thicker and create a little "hill" or raised section for the mushrooms to sit on.

19. **Continue stabbing on a few new layers at a time** until you like the shape.

Attach the mushrooms to the foundation.

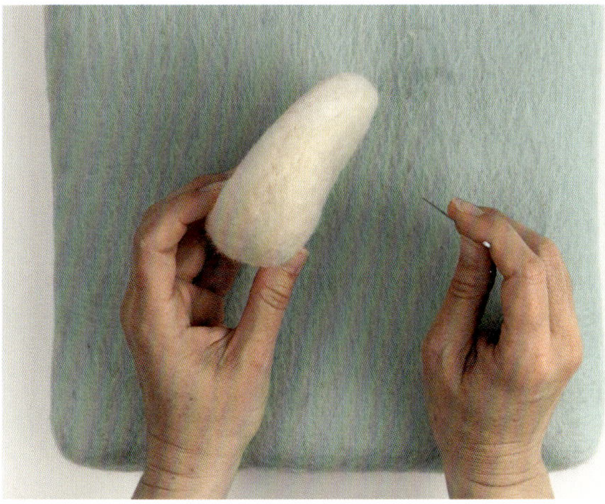

20. **Step back and examine your foundation;** it should look similar to this when finished. When you sit it in front of you, you want it to be higher in the back and lower in the front. The mushrooms will sit on this little incline. Continue poking until the whole thing holds its shape and is nice and firm.

21. **Open up the fibers at the bottom of the stems.**

22. **Spread the opened fibers onto the foundation and poke into them.** Poke deep into the bottom of the stems through to the foundation and attach all the unfelted wool. Arrange the mushrooms together in a visually pleasing way on the little hill.

23. **Cover the whole foundation up with dark-brown wool.** Use large pieces for faster coverage if you have them, but you can also overlap smaller pieces until the whole thing is covered. There is no need to do the bottom, since that won't be seen.

Mushrooms and Moss

Add the moss.

24. To make the moss, **tear off tiny thin pieces of green wool and roll them back and forth on your palm,** as if you're making a tiny "snake" with clay. The ends should become pointy. It can help to keep your hands moist with a damp sponge or washcloth. Make lots of these.

25. When you are ready to put them on, **fold each little piece in half,** forming what looks like two tiny blades of grass, or bits of moss.

26. To attach the moss to the "soil," **poke down through the folded part into the dark-brown wool.** Leave the ends sticking up. Sometimes it helps to hold the ends upright with one hand while you are poking down into the middle fold with your needle. Add lots of these in clumps or swathes, until you like the look of your scene.

Finish it up.

27. Take some pieces of green wool and spread them out over the brown wool on the front edge of the scene. Poke these down until they are smooth and attached.

Pretty Pumpkins

Pumpkins are such a fun thing to make and display. Stick them in a bowl or a centerpiece when autumn begins. They never go out of style. Over the years I have acquired different types of handmade pumpkins, but needle-felted pumpkins are my favorite. They are really an ideal first needle felting project if you want to learn to make small sculptures. I prefer to leave mine unadorned, but you can add faces and leaves if you want to.

These pictures show how to make three pumpkins that are slightly different in size and shape. To make more pumpkins and vary them further, use the same techniques but make your rolls with more or less core wool and then use a wider variety of colors.

SUPPLIES

This amount of wool will make three pumpkins. If you want to make more, simply start with more wool. Each pumpkin uses about ⅓ oz. of core wool and ⅛ oz. of dyed wool.

- 1 oz. core wool batting
- ⅛ oz. of roving in the following colors: orange, peach, and gold
- 1-inch pieces of felted wool yarn
- 38 Triangle felting needles
- a mat to use as a work surface

Pretty Pumpkins

Prepare the pumpkin shapes.

1. **Tear the core wool into three long strips.** Each one will become a pumpkin. Try for widths of approximately 1½, 2½, and 3½ inches (3.8, 6.4, and 8.9 cm). The width of the strip will become the height of the pumpkin. If your core wool is thicker, you may need to stretch it out. If thinner, you may end up with two strips per pumpkin.

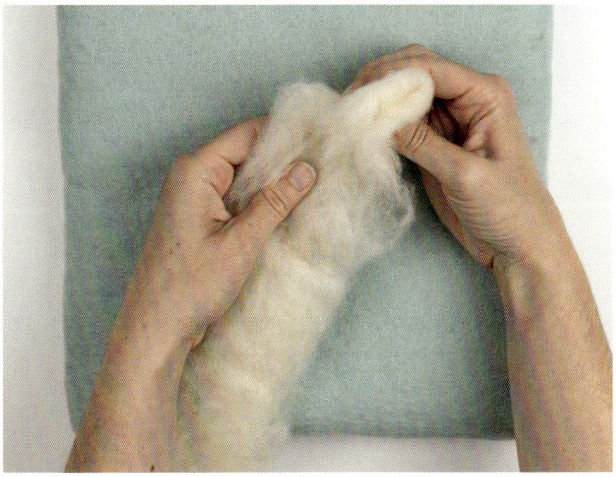

2. To start rolling a pumpkin shape, **pinch the wool together** so that there will be extra wool in the middle. Then start folding toward you, keeping the wool pulled snug.

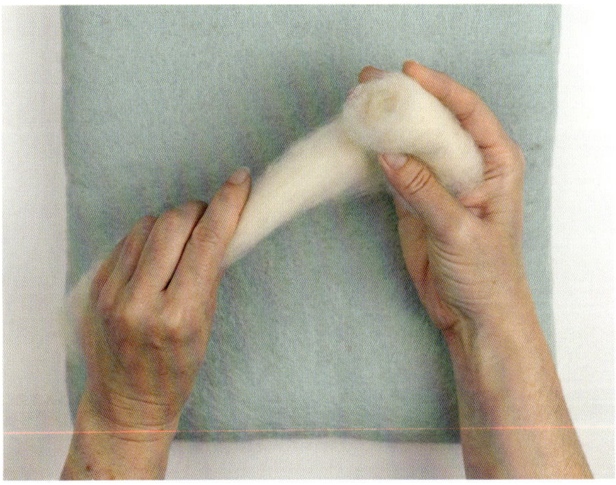

3. **Keep the strip of wool squished together and / or gently pull it out to narrow it;** this way, as you fold up the shape, more wool will be concentrated around the middle of the pumpkin. Unroll the wool and try again if your pumpkin shape ends up too tall and thin.

4. If you need to add another strip to complete a pumpkin shape, **just start wrapping it around and keep going.**

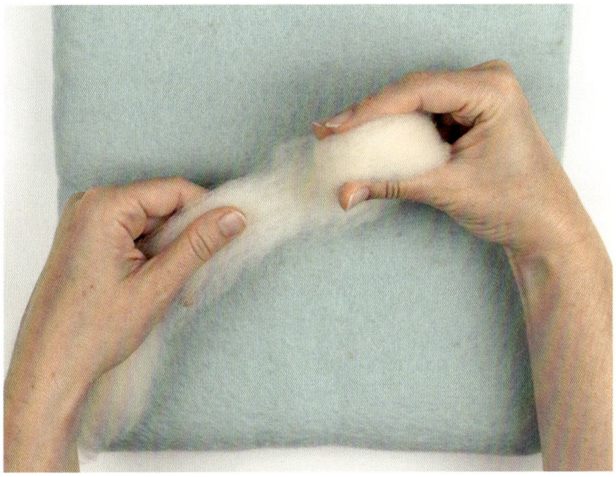

5. For the shortest pumpkin, **be sure to keep the wool compacted when you roll it,** so that the pumpkin ends up wider and shorter than the others.

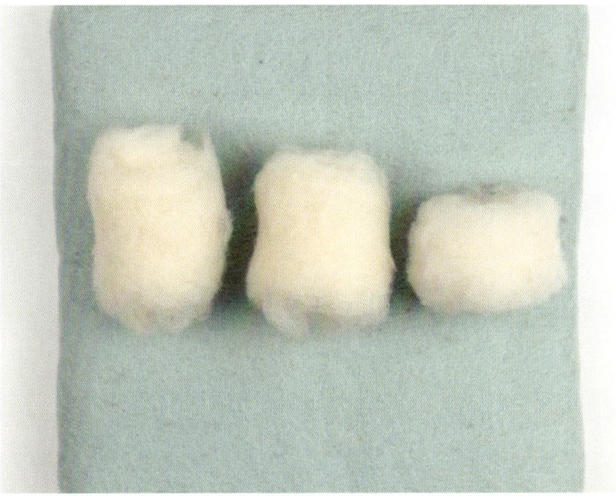

6. **Your finished rolls should look like this.** If you want to change their shapes at this point, you can unroll them and move wool from one to another and reroll. They should be snug but with a little give, so that you'll be able to easily make the indented ribs.

Felt the pumpkin shape.

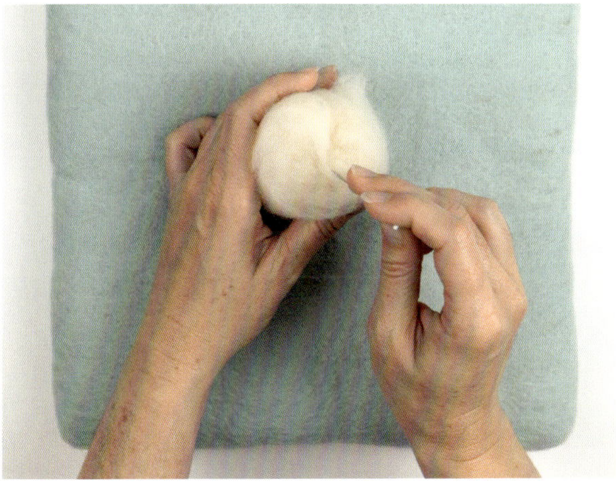

7. **Place the medium-sized roll on the mat and start poking it with the needle.** First, work on the top and bottom by moving the outer layers of wool toward the middle and poking them down. While starting the shape, stab in far with the needle. About half of the needle should be going into the wool.

8. **Continue shaping.** The angle that you stab is the direction in which you will push and compact the wool. Poke from each end toward the center, to keep more wool pushed toward the middle of the pumpkin. Work all around the pumpkin a few times, shaping gradually and keeping your pokes about ½ inch (1.3 cm) apart.

Pretty Pumpkins

9. **Continue poking until the pumpkin is holding its shape.** It should be a little bit firm but still able to be squished in if you squeeze it. This bit of give will allow you to add the "ribs" later.

Add color to the outside.

10. **Tear off pieces of roving and wrap them around the shape,** putting the ends on the top and bottom of the pumpkin. Overlap each piece slightly so that the core wool doesn't show through. Poke gently to attach the pieces to the core wool, going in less deeply with the needle than when you were creating the shape.

Add the ribs.

11. **Once the whole pumpkin is covered, start putting on the "ribs."** The first indent is a line that goes all the way around the pumpkin, dividing it into two segments. Poke in deep with the needle for this part, going over the same line multiple times until there is a good indent.

12. **Look for gaps.** If at any point you see any spots where core wool is showing through, you can take a small extra piece of roving (if you have one left over), put it over the thin spot, and poke it on. It will blend right in. If you don't have extra roving, try to push roving into the thin spot from either side of it.

13. **Add another indented line that runs all the way around the pumpkin.** This one should be perpendicular to the first line, dividing the pumpkin into four fairly even segments.

14. **Add more indented lines, dividing each of the four segments in half,** so that the pumpkin ends up with eight segments. Continue stabbing these lines more, if needed, until they are all evenly indented.

Finish the surface.

15. **Finish each segment.** Poke gently with the needle so that it pushes wool away from each rib toward the middle of the segment. After you do one side of the segment, flip the pumpkin around and do the other side. Poking with your stabs close together and at a shallow, even depth helps to smooth the surface.

TIP

As you finish each segment as described in step 15, go back over the ribs on each side of the segment by stabbing in far again. The finishing process condenses the wool a bit on each segment, leading to ribs that are not as deep. You can go back and stab more on the ribs as many times as you need to, to maintain good pumpkin shaping.

Add the stem.

16. When all segments are finished and smooth, **choose a stem piece.** Open up and spread out the fibers at the bottom of the stem, to make it easier to attach to the pumpkin.

17. **Spread about a ¼ inch (6 mm) of stem fibers onto the top of the pumpkin.** Hold the stem in place while you poke in deeply around the bottom until it is well attached.

18. **Trim the stem as desired.** Use the same process to complete the other pumpkins. The amount of wool you use and the way that you roll it up in the beginning will naturally make their shapes slightly different.

Candle Wreath

Fall is a beautiful time of year where I live, with all the leaves in hues of rust, vibrant reds, oranges, and golden yellows. I love to gather acorn tops on my walks in the crisp air while I relish the crunch of leaves underfoot. This wreath is inspired by these autumn days. Something about gathering acorn tops makes me feel like a kid in search of treasure, pleased when I find a really nice one and can plop it into my pocket. These acorn tops will adorn felted balls, a simple yet cute decoration. I also find that making colorful leaves on a felt backing is an easy and satisfying project. I have turned them into a candle wreath here, but they can also be used in garlands or simply strewn about loose on a table or mantel.

SUPPLIES

- 8-by-12-inch (20.3 by 30.5 cm) piece of rust-red 100% wool felt
- ⅛ oz. pieces of wool batting in the following colors: dark red, bright red, yellow, orange, and green
- 5 acorn tops
- 38 Star felting needles
- 1 6-inch grapevine wreath
- craft glue or hot glue
- a thin permanent marker
- a sharp pair of scissors
- pattern templates (see page 157)
- a mat to use as a work surface

Candle Wreath

Cut out the pattern.

1. Make extra copies so that you have two of the larger leaves and three of the slightly smaller ones. It is easier to trace them onto the felt by using all five leaves, since there is not much extra room.

Trace the leaves.

2. Use a thin permanent marker or fabric marker to trace the leaf outlines on the felt. There should be just enough room for the five leaves.

Cut out the leaves.

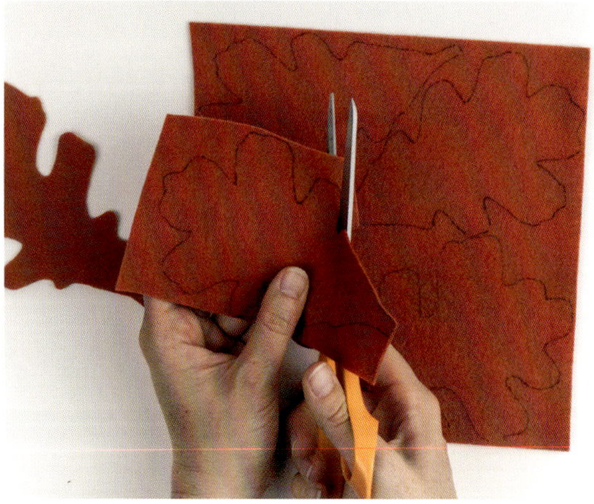

3. Cut out the leaf shapes with a sharp pair of fabric scissors.

Add color.

4. Pull off pieces of colored wool and lay it out on the leaves. Each one should be a little different from the others. Use the picture here as a guide, or find real leaves or pictures of real leaves in the fall to use as inspiration.

TIP

As you lay out the wool on each leaf, try to keep the wool fibers going in a similar direction. I find that fibers lying mostly vertically look best on leaves. Overlap each tuft of wool a little bit so that the colors blend together where they meet.

5. **Put a leaf on the mat and start poking it.** Use the needle to pull wool onto the leaf at the edges where it sticks out before you poke it down. If you see any spots where the felt is showing through, you can add more wool to cover it up. Continue stabbing until the wool is flat and attached to the leaf.

Make the veins.

6. **To put the veins on the leaf, use a leaf pattern as a general guide.** First, pull off a thin strip of yellow wool.

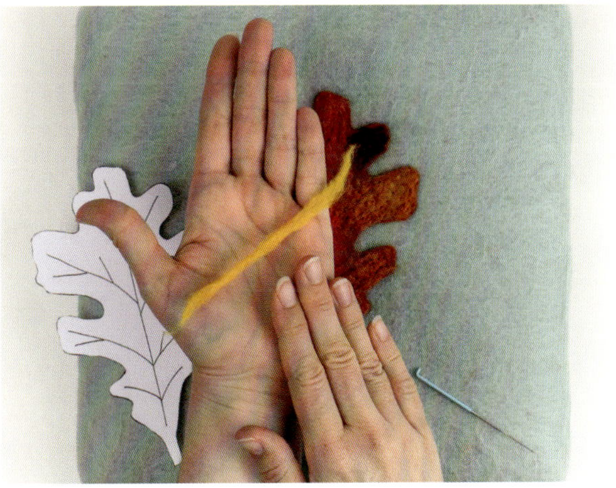

7. **Roll the wool back and forth on your palm,** as though you're making a "snake" out of clay. This condenses the wool and helps it hold together.

8. **Start putting on veins, one at a time.** Start at the top of the leaf, or near any edge. Poke on the end of the yellow wool to attach it and then hold the vein in place with one hand while you poke with the other hand directly on the line. Poking at an angle on the edges of the lines helps make them straight and tidy.

9. **Continue putting on veins.** If you put the middle one on first, the rest connect to that. You can overlap the wool slightly anywhere the veins join. Pull off extra wool right past the overlap so that the veins don't get too thick.

Finish the leaves.

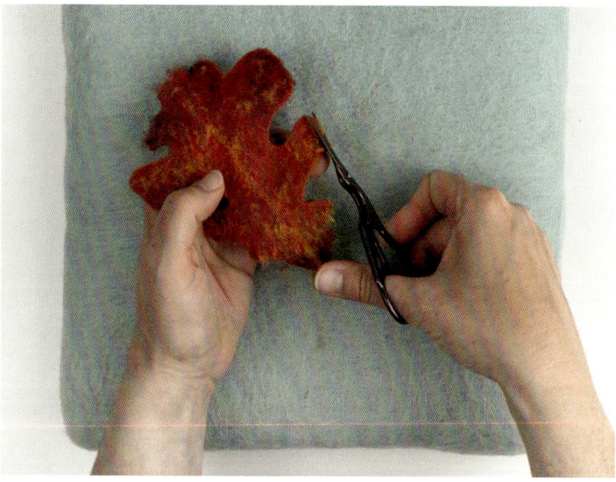

10. **When you are happy with the leaf, pull it up off the mat.** It can take some tugging, but don't worry; it will be okay!

11. **Trim any extra fibers that are sticking out at the edges.** You can even trim the back a little bit if you want. I find that smaller scissors work best for trimming.

Glue the leaves on the wreath.

12. Arrange the leaves. After you're sure that you like their placement, glue them on. I use a little bit of hot glue, but other glue can be substituted. You need only a few dots of glue—just enough to hold the leaves to the wreath.

Make the acorns.

13. Make little felted balls that will become acorns. These are made the same way as the balls on the Carrot Garland (page 55), except they are smaller. Tear a thin strip of wool a little less than 1 inch (2.5 cm) wide and 4 inches (10.2 cm) long and roll that up. Then take another strip about the same size and roll in the opposite direction.

14. Put the ball on the mat and start poking it, being careful of your other fingers. Shaping small balls goes quickly. Turn the ball often and try to work on it gradually to keep it round. Poke in more on any parts that are popped out and less on parts that are already narrower or indented.

15. Keep poking until the ball is firm and round. Test it periodically with the acorn cap that will go on top. If the ball is still too big for the cap, poke more to make the ball smaller. Poke with shallow stabs close together when you are ready to smooth the surface.

Candle Wreath

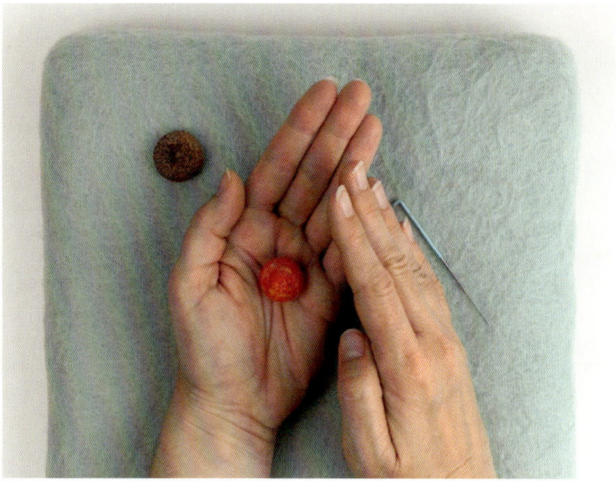

16. Roll the ball around on your palm to make it rounder and smoother. Using water to keep your hands moist or even wet when you do this can be helpful.

Put on the caps.

17. Secure the acorn cap onto the ball, using hot glue or craft glue. One big dot of glue will do it.

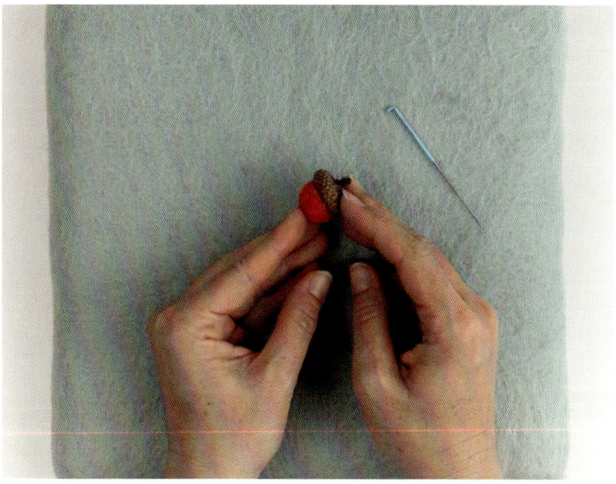

18. Hold the acorn cap on the ball until the glue starts to dry enough that it won't come off. Make one acorn in each color of wool and then arrange them around the wreath when you display it, or glue them onto the wreath if you prefer.

WINTER

Festive Ornaments

When I was a kid, my mom hosted ornament-making parties. Friends and family who enjoyed crafting would gather to make homemade ornaments while Christmas music played in the background. Sometimes we made them from colored dough and other times from craft felt. One year we made a bunch of God's Eyes with toothpicks and embroidery floss. Our Christmas tree held tons of handmade ornaments, all displayed together against a backdrop of colored lights and gold tinsel, whether they matched or not. It wasn't decorated with a theme or color scheme in mind but was about remembering time spent together. When I started needle felting, naturally I made felted ornaments! Of all my kit designs, these classic baubles have remained the most popular, year in and year out. I hope you enjoy creating them. Perhaps you'll even want to host an ornament-making party of your own!

SUPPLIES

- 4 wool ornament blanks (you could also make your own balls using the same techniques shown in Carrot Garland, using approximately ⅓ oz. core wool per ball)
- ¼ oz. pieces of wool batting in the following colors: olive green and cranberry red
- 38 Twisted felting needles
- 64 inches of string (I used DMC Pearl Cotton in Winter White)
- a 3-inch doll needle
- 4 "ornament caps" cut from gray felted wool yarn
- a mat to use as a work surface (optional)

Prepare the balls.

1. **Poke each ball for five to ten minutes** to make it rounder and firmer before you decorate it. Poke more on areas that are popped out. Poke less on areas that are squished in. Do not poke so hard that the ball gets hard; it should still have a little give to it. If you do not have access to preformed balls, you can make your own.

Decorate ornament 1.

2. **Tear a long, thin strip of green wool.** Gently stretch this out over the ball, keeping it straight around the middle. Poke one small section at a time and then stretch and place the next section until you've gone all the way around. Overlap the ends. Use small pieces of wool to fill in any thin spots to keep the line an even width.

3. **Put in another line running perpendicular to the first** and wrap it all the way around the ball. To keep the edges straight and tidy, gently pull wool into place with the tip of the needle and poke it down. Poking the edges of the line from a side angle can help smooth it out and tuck in any stray fibers.

4. **Put on two more green lines that wrap all the way around the ball,** dividing it into eight even sections. I think of this like adding a plus sign on the top of the ball and then adding another one diagonal to the first. It is okay if the ball gets indented where these lines are; that will be fixed at the end.

5. **Use pieces of red to make marquise (pointed oval) shapes in the spaces between the lines.** Start poking at the point, gently dragging the wool into place with the needle. Add more wool to round out the sides if needed. Poke on these until they are smooth and well attached to the ball.

Finish it up.

6. When you are happy with the design, **poke all over the white parts to make the ball round again.** The places with color added are usually indented. Stab in hard if you need to change the shape of the ball but then stab in gently, near the surface, with your pokes close together to make it smoother. This will be the final step for each ornament.

Decorate ornament 2.

7. **To make the next ball, make a green line around it, as in step 2.** Then add leaves in pairs that connect to the line. To make a leaf, tear a thin little strip of green wool and bend it in half. The curved top will be the top of the leaf. Try to make these about the size that you want the leaves to become.

8. **Start poking the leaf where it joins the line.** Then pull the wool up into a point, or a rounded end. Leaves should go up diagonally from the line. They will all look a little different from each other, but that is okay. It helps the ornament look handmade.

9. To make the red dots that go in the middle of each set of leaves, **take a small piece of red wool and roll it on your palm to make it round.** Alternately, you can work with it in your fingers and fold it into a circle.

10. **Add a red dot in the middle of each pair of leaves.** To keep the dots round when you put them on, poke the edges first. Pull the wool gently into place with the needle and then poke it down. You can pull off any leaves and dots you don't like and try again.

11. **Place a green dot in the middle of the bottom of the ornament.**

12. **Roll a thin strip of red wool on your palm until it holds together.** Then, form a circle with it around the green dot. It can be challenging to keep it round as you stab it on, but work slowly and remember it will still look good if it is not perfect!

13. Once you have attached the red circle around the dot, **add small leaves around the circle.** There should be room for around seven of them. Repeat this same design on the top of the ornament once you have finished it on the bottom.

Decorate ornament 3.

14. To make the next ball, **start the same as you did with the first ornament, making two lines that wrap around it as in step 3.** Then start putting green circles on these lines. Make those the same way you made red dots for the leaf ornament.

15. Once you have green circles added to the lines, **make a red diamond in each white section.** There will be four diamonds on the ornament. Pull off pieces of red wool to make the shape of each diamond.

16. **Try to keep the lines straight and pull the wool in place with the needle before you poke it down.** Use the same techniques from previous ornaments when you are making the lines.

17. Once your diamond is complete, **place a green line down the middle.**

18. **Put three green circles on the line.** Make the other three sides of the ornament in the same way.

Decorate ornament 4.

19. **Tear a piece of red wool that will become a circle on the top of the final ornament.** Fold the edges under to make it rounder. Lay this on the top of the ornament, keeping it centered.

20. **Poke the edges of the circle first,** pushing and pulling the wool gently with the needle to move it into place, then poke it down. After the edges are finished, poke the rest of the circle until it is flattened on the ball. Add small pieces of red if there are any thin spots where you see white showing through.

21. **Tear a green strip of wool and wrap it around the ornament** to make a thick stripe under the red circle. Use extra pieces at the edges if any spots are thinner, to make it an even width.

22. **Next, tear another strip of green and make a thinner green stripe around the ball,** leaving a band of white in between the stripes. Then add a red stripe below the thin green one, then a green stripe directly below it, but touching this time.

23. **At the bottom of the ball, add one more red circle,** similar to the one on the top of the ball. Make it whatever size looks the best on your ball once you have the other stripes on; it doesn't need to be the same size as the one on top.

Add the string and ornament caps.

24. To add an ornament cap, **cut the string into four pieces,** each approximately 16 inches (40.6 cm) long. Thread a piece of string onto the doll needle, leaving a tail. Then thread the ornament cap on the needle and pull it over the needle onto the string.

25. Insert the needle into the center point of the ornament from the top, pushing the needle all the way through the ornament, out through the center point at the bottom.

26. Go back into the center point of the ornament from the bottom and up and out through the top. Pass the needle right next to where you went in and out on the first pass, but not in the exact same holes.

27. Pass the needle back through the ornament cap, then move the cap down onto the top of the ornament.

28. Finish the ornament. Hold the two ends of the string together, tie a knot a few inches above the ornament cap, and then cut off any extra string.

Pine Cone Stockings

In the world of natural fibers, the one I like best after wool has to be linen. This project blends both: a linen stocking and a simple pine cone pattern needle-felted with wool. If you are not a sewist and have trouble finding a linen stocking, check the website Etsy. A felt stocking could also work for this project. Stencils are another widely available, crafty tool that can be used for needle felting. If your stencil is not exactly like the one shown for this project, that is okay! You can adapt the project to the stencil(s) you have. Alphabet stencils can also be handy if you want to add a name.

Note: If you don't have stencils on hand, photocopy the pattern on page 158, transfer it to a piece of cardstock, and cut the design out with an X-ACTO knife.

SUPPLIES

- linen stocking
- ⅛ oz. pieces of wool batting in the following colors: olive green and dark brown
- pine cone and pine branch stencil (or card stock and X-ACTO knife)
- alphabet stencils (optional)
- 38 Star felting needles
- 4 straight pins
- a small foam or wool mat that can fit into the stocking

Pine Cone Stockings

Get the mat and stencil into place.

1. **If you are going to make multiple stockings, make each slightly different.** Branches should start at the top and hang down diagonally to the right or left. Pine cones should hang straight down or point slightly to the right or left. To start, put the mat into the stocking, under where you want to place a branch or pine cone.

2. **Insert straight pins in three or four spots on the outer edge of the shape you are using** so that the stencil won't move around as you work. It helps if the pins have a ball on top. These should be pushed through the fabric down into the mat.

Fill in the greenery.

3. **Tear off little pieces of wool and start filling in the stencil.** Try to tear pieces that will fit into the spaces you want to fill, but it is okay if they are slightly bigger, since the wool will compact and some of it will go through to the backside of the fabric.

4. **Place the wool inside the stencil and start poking straight down into it with the needle,** stabbing through the fabric and slightly into the mat. Try not to stab into the stencil itself because you will risk breaking or bending your needle, but it will happen sometimes.

5. **Continue filling in, piece by piece,** until the whole shape is filled in with wool. The wool should be flattened out and well attached to the fabric before you pull up the stencil. If the wool still seems fuzzy, continue poking it.

Finish it up.

6. **Take off the pins and pull the stencil off the stocking.** Clean up the design by using the needle to gently pull any fibers that are sticking up at the edges into the wool-covered area, and poke them down. If you notice any thin areas that need to be more filled in with extra wool, add pieces of wool to those.

7. **When you are happy with the design, pull it up off the mat.** This can take some tugging. Check one more time after it is off the mat, since the fiber tends to loosen up slightly. You can always put the mat back underneath and work on it more if needed.

Add a pinecone.

8. **Pick the next element you want to add and repeat the process.** When filling in pine cones, it may be helpful to roll the fiber around on your palm or in between your fingers a little bit before you poke it down, since most of the areas to be filled in are round.

9. **Use as many pieces of wool as you need in each tiny area to be filled in,** until the whole thing is covered with wool.

10. **Refine the shapes.** Pine cones can look fuzzy and need to be tidied up as well once the stencil is off. This is normal.

Keep adding more pieces of the design.

11. **Spend more time pulling wool into place,** moving it from the edges into the middle of each area and stabbing it down until it is flatter, with better-defined fabric areas in between the filled-in parts.

12. **Try to use all branch and pine cone elements on the stocking.** When you are happy with the design, an optional last step is to add a name at the top; 1½-inch (3.8 cm) alphabet stencils work well for short names. Use 1-inch (2.5 cm) alphabet stencils for longer names.

Mountain Cabin

Recently I've started experimenting with needle felting projects that combine 2-D and 3-D elements. This is one of those projects. Using a wool "foundation" is another idea that came to me after I had already been felting for a long time. A foundation is the same as a wool mat, but instead of taking the project off at the end, you build the project to stay put, and the foundation becomes part of the finished piece. This solves some mounting issues, especially when you want to place 3-D elements on a 2-D picture or help top-heavy shapes stand up. With a wool foundation, you can simply stab the pieces of your project on without having to think about sewing or gluing. Because the foundation is wool, it will accept the rest of the needle-felted parts that you want to attach to it.

SUPPLIES

- ½ oz. core wool batting
- ⅛ oz. pieces of wool batting in the following colors: pale blue, gray, forest green, and white
- 1/16 oz. pieces of wool batting in dark red, dark brown, and blue green
- 7 inch square wool "foundation"
- 38 Triangle felting needles

Mountain Cabin

Put in the sky.

1. **Stretch light-blue wool over the top of the foundation** and poke it all over until it is well attached and flattened out. Make sure you place the wool with enough to wrap around the top and sides.

2. **Wrap the wool around to the back side.** Poke the wool flat on the sides, as well, so that they look finished when you display the piece. Poke the ends of the wool on the back so that they stay in place, but otherwise, don't worry about the appearance of the back.

Add the mountains.

3. **Lay out pieces of gray wool to be the mountains.** Make three mountain peaks. Use two or three pieces of wool per mountain and have them overlap each other.

4. **Poke down the gray wool.** Fold under the edges of the wool where the mountains meet the sky, and angle the needle into the backside of the wool as you tack down the edges to keep them thick enough to cover the sky. Then poke straight down on the rest of the gray wool once the edges are finished.

5. **Make the mountains slightly 3-D** by putting on more pieces of wool and then poking these down gently. You still want the wool to be felted, but don't flatten it out completely. The places you build up with more wool will have more dimension.

6. **Continue poking until the mountains look similar to this.** You can add extra wool pieces more than once if you need to as you are building up an area.

Add the treeline.

7. To make the treeline, **stretch a piece of forest-green wool across the bottom of the mountains,** overlapping them slightly. Pull it so it dips down a little in the middle. Fold under the top edge and work on the edge line first to keep it smooth before poking all over the rest of the forest-green wool.

8. **Use small tufts of forest-green wool to make little points on the top edge of the treeline.** This helps it look more like trees in the distance. Vary their size and shape so that they don't all look the same. This will mimic nature. Add some slightly bigger tufts in the middle of the green wool, to depict more tree outlines.

Mountain Cabin

Put in a snow-covered hill.

9. **Start building up a snowy hill at the bottom with pieces of core wool.** These should be big enough to stretch across the whole piece. You will need a few layers, depending on the thickness of your core wool.

10. **Make the hill a bit higher at the right side,** and make it dip a little lower on the left side. Simply add some smaller pieces of core wool at the right side to build up the hill. Stab into this with the needle until it firms up everywhere. The direction you stab in with the needle will push the wool into the contour you want.

11. Once you are happy with the shaping and firmness of the hill, **cover it with white wool and then poke that down to attach it.** Poke more gently now, to create a smooth surface. Stabs that go in about ¼ inch (6 mm) and are close together help with smoothing.

Add snowcaps to the mountains.

12. **Add snowcaps** by pulling off small pieces of white wool and arranging them where they will go.

13. **Push and pull the wool into place with the needle.** At the edges, stab in at an angle, tucking wool in and making the edges tidy and crisp. Continue until all of the snow is attached. Pull it up and move it around or add more pieces of white if needed until you are happy with it.

Make the cabin.

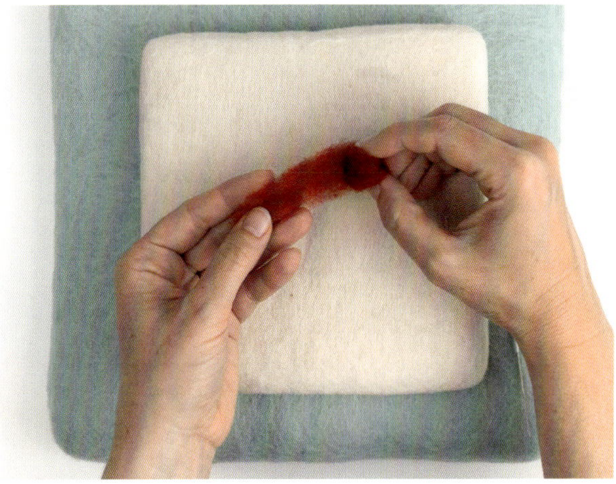

14. **Roll up a strip of red wool that will become the little cabin.** This should be snug but still have give to it, so that you can manipulate its shape as you are felting.

15. **Poke into the top of the roll of wool from each side,** flattening it out and making the angled roofline but keeping a point in the middle. Poke straight in on the bottom to make a flat base for the cabin.

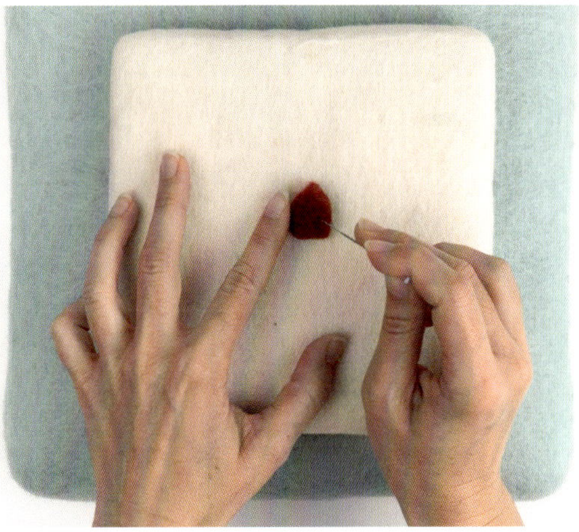

16. **Turn the cabin as you poke it gently from each side.** Create four flat sides, similar to dice. The bottom should be flat and the roof angled, making a tiny 3-D house shape. There is no need to poke much at the corners. Concentrate on flattening each side, and corners will form naturally.

17. **Make two roof pieces by folding two little strips of brown wool up** so that they are two to three layers thick. Also tear a little piece of brown wool that will become the door. Start felting the tiny roof pieces. These should be firm and hold together before you put them on the cabin.

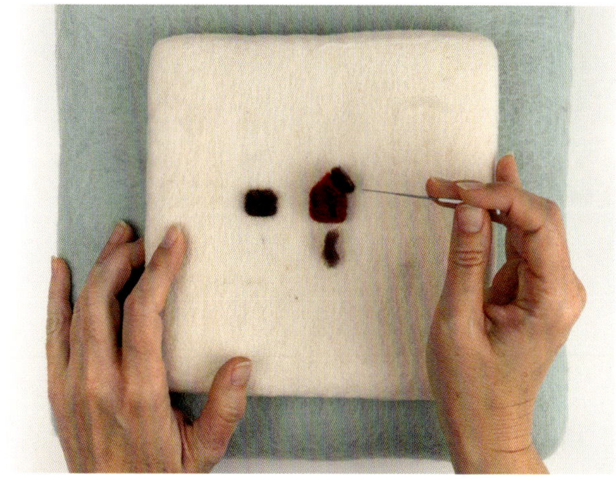

18. Once the roof pieces are felted, **attach them to the cabin by poking through the pieces and into the cabin.** You can also poke the edges of the roof gently into the red of the cabin at the places where they need to join.

TIP

When adding very tiny details such as the door, it is important to use a very small piece of wool. Poke the edges first, starting at the corners, to get the shaping right. Pull the wool gently into place with the tip of the needle before you poke it down, with the end shape in mind. It is not necessary to stab in deeply at all; work mostly on the surface. Be sure you have good lighting when you're working on small details. A magnifying tool, such as a magnifying task lamp, can also be helpful.

Create some tiny pine trees.

19. Once the two roof pieces are attached, if they don't line up perfectly, **add a small amount of wool to the ridgeline where they meet;** this will join them and help them hold together. Then add the door.

20. **Make little trees by taking strips of blue-green wool and rolling them up,** working to form the wool into a bit of a point at the top. These will end up looking like little cone shapes.

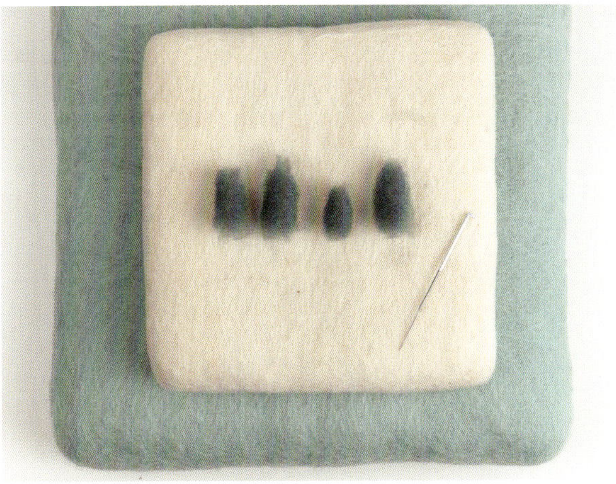

21. **Make four tree rolls, varying their sizes.**

22. **Start stabbing into the trees and working on them while they are attached to the mat.** Once their shapes are holding together, pick each one up and stab into it from the other sides as well until each one is firm. Finally, poke gently at the surface to give them a smooth look before you attach them to the piece.

Mountain Cabin

Attach the cabin and trees.

23. Add the cabin to the hillside, stabbing in deep with the needle to catch the bottom of the cabin and push some of its wool down into the hill. Stab around the bottom edge of the cabin until it is holding on.

24. Add the trees in the same way, stabbing deep through their bottom edges down into the hill. I like to put one tree by the cabin and arrange the other three in a little clump on the left side of the cabin.

Add some snowflakes.

25. Tear off very tiny pieces of white wool and roll these around on your palm and in between your fingers until they form little balls. Stab these on with a few deep and deliberate stabs around their edges. Don't stab directly in the middle of the snowflake, or it can get buried in the sky.

Where to Go from Here

Needle felting is such a fun and satisfying art form. It warms my heart when a customer tells me that needle felting has changed their life for the better and given them a creative outlet that they love. Sometimes they are writing to say how much needle felting has meant to a loved one while they are going through treatment or recovering from a surgery. Teens and young adults can benefit too. It can be a great stress reliever and a way to get off screens for some quiet self-time.

I hope that the projects and information in this book will propel you into the wonderful world of needle felting and bring beauty to your home in the process. Handmade decorations are always extra special. I know it brings a smile to my face every time I take out our family's homemade decorations and display them for another holiday season. Felting parties for making eggs, pumpkins, or ornaments are also a great way to make memories with friends and family.

With each year that goes by, needle felting continues to evolve as an art form. New artists are always coming up with unique creations that are different from anything I've ever seen. Whether you simply enjoy the projects in this book or become one of those artists, I hope needle felting is a delightful addition to your life.

♡ Elizabeth

Resources

There are new needle-felting suppliers, artists, and teachers coming onto the scene all the time, and there are so many now that I can't keep track of them all. Therefore, this is not meant to be a comprehensive list, but a starting point if you are looking for businesses who sell top-quality supplies, teachers who are well loved, and some of my favorite artists to check out for needle felting inspiration.

WHERE TO BUY SUPPLIES

UNITED STATES

Felted Sky (the author's needle felting shop): www.feltedsky.com. Here you will find all the supplies used in this book and plenty more!
Living Felt: www.livingfelt.com
Sarafina Fiber Art: www.sarafinafiberart.com
Bear Creek Felting: www.bearcreekfelting.com
Weir Crafts: www.weircrafts.com
The Woolery: www.woolery.com
The Felted Ewe: www.thefeltedewe.com
Grey Fox Felting: www.greyfoxfelting.com

EUROPE

Dyeing House Gallery: www.dhgshop.it
World of Wool: www.worldofwool.co.uk
Meaningful Crafts: www.meaningfulcrafts.com

NEEDLE FELTING ARTISTS WHO TEACH

Dani Ives: www.daniives.com
Erin Gardner: www.greyfoxfelting.com
Sara Renzulli: www.sarafinafiberart.com
Teresa Perleberg: www.bearcreekfelting.com
Sophie Wheatley: www.feltandbeautiful.co.uk
Jaana Mattson: www.jaanamattson.com
Megan Nedds: www.etsy.com/shop/TheWoolenWagon
Michelle Onderstall: www.fudgeandmabel.co.uk
Tracy Turner: @birdie_and_blossom

MORE ARTISTS TO WATCH

Andrea Love: @andreaanimates
Sarah Ritchie: www.sarah-ritchie.com
Amy Reader: www.amyreaderartist.com
Heather Talbot: @api_artist
Simon Brown: @thegentlemanfelter
Eugenya: @wools_symphony
Hanna and Olha Dovhan: @manooni_shop
Nastasya Shulyak: @stowaways_toys
Stephanie Metz: www.stephaniemetz.com
Katherine McLelland: www.katmcclelland.com
Kiyoshi Mino: @kiyoshiminofelt
Jo Hobbs: www.curlyjocreation.com

Pattern Templates

All patterns are 100% to size unless otherwise specified.

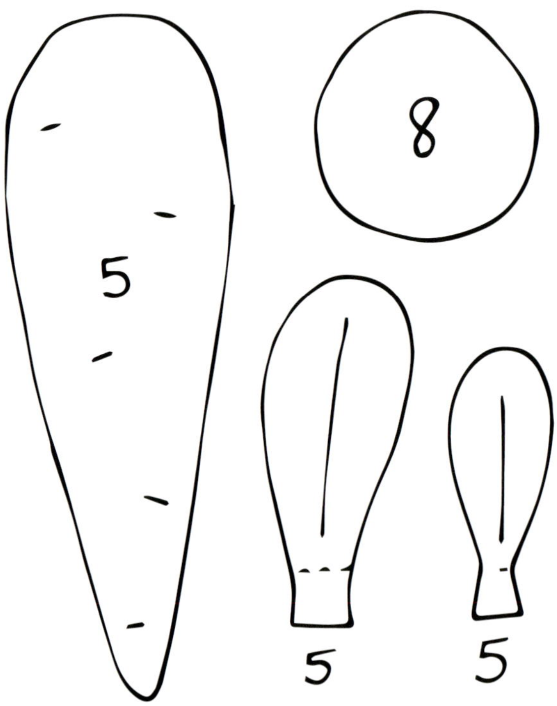

Carrot Garland pattern, project found on page 54

Spring Tulips pattern, project found on page 62

Pattern Templates

All patterns are 100% to size unless otherwise specified.

◀ Moonstone Succulent pattern, project found on page 72

▶ Citrus Coasters pattern, project found on page 88

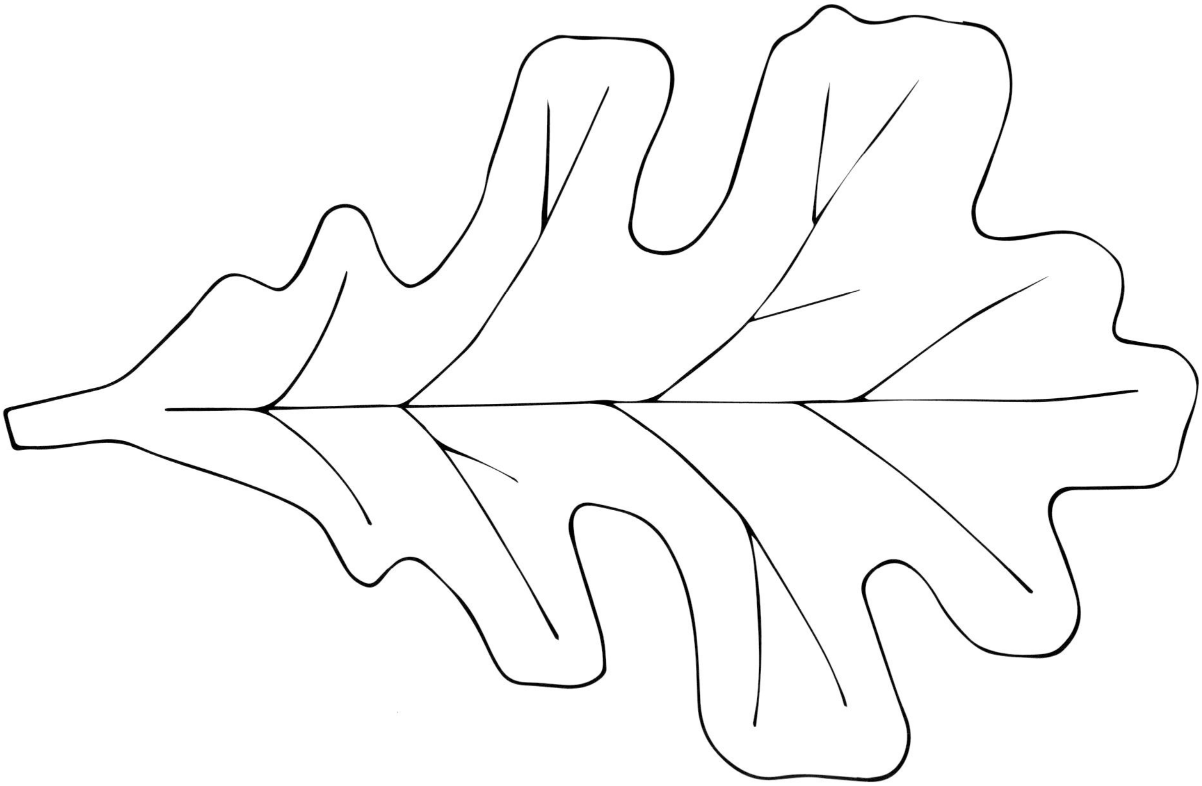

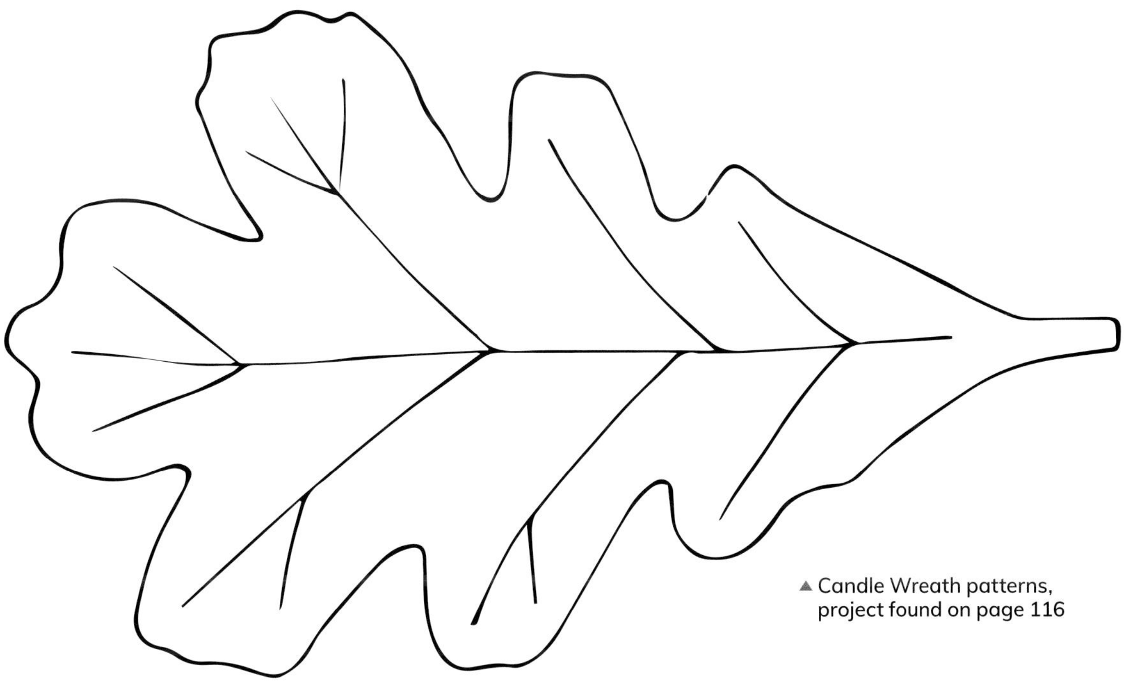

▲ Candle Wreath patterns, project found on page 116

Pattern Templates

All patterns are 100% to size unless otherwise specified.

▲ Pine Cone Stockings pattern, project found on page 136

ABOUT THE AUTHOR

Elizabeth Whitton is a self-taught fiber artist who turned her love of wool into a thriving needle felting business called Felted Sky. She has a knack for designing and teaching beautiful small projects and helping new felters to fall in love with the art form. Her kits and carefully curated supplies can be found online and in many small shops across the US and beyond. Elizabeth enjoys teaching through her kits, in person, and online. She loves that she has been able to promote stress relief, creativity, and joy through needle felting.